MW01204020

A SUMMER OF FEAR

Rebecca Patrick-Howard

Want FREE audio books and ebooks? To be the first to find out about new releases? Exclusive content? Sign up for Rebecca's newsletter today. Don't worry, Rebecca won't spam you. She's not into potted meat...

http://eepurl.com/Srwkn

Copyright © 2014 by Rebecca Patrick-Howard
Published by Mistletoe Press
All rights reserved. No part of this book may be reproduced, scanned, or
distributed in any printed or electronic form without permission.

First Edition: September 2014
Printed in the United States of America
www.rebeccaphoward.net

Disclaimer:

The following events are true. However, names, place names, and identifying factors have been changed.

For Dilly and Alabama

Book Map

Arrival

pulled up to the resort beaten, battered, and cold. It was a sixteen-hour drive and I'd gone from the unseasonably sweltering spring heat of Kentucky to the foggy, murky chill of New England. Somewhere along the way I'd managed to pick up a sinus infection; my nose was running, my head throbbed, and my throat was raw.

The resort, nearly five miles off the main road, was isolated and secluded from the rest of the world. The gravel road threw up a spray of white dust on my decrepit navy blue Buick as I slowly wound through the trees that towered above me, going deep into a tunnel of brown and green. I wasn't due for another day, but I wanted to find my destination first. I was shocked Mapquest had brought me this far.

The long, rambling road was eerily quiet. There wouldn't have been room for another car to drive past me, but the length of the road coupled with the slow speed I had to take it with only amplified my solitude. I was completely alone in the dim tunnel, wisps of fog reaching out to me through the thick clusters of trees and curling around my tires and even slithering in through the vents. I turned Emmylou Harris and John Denver up on the CD player to lighten the mood, but not even "Wild Montana Skies" helped; the tune sounded hollow and distant.

The Minnetonka Resort (not its real name) in the small New Hampshire mountain town had hired me over the phone to be its office manager for the summer. I was twenty-five years old and had the choice of two other jobs (Colorado and Texas) but settled on this one because it paid the best and was close to Boston. Unlike the other places, the hiring director of this one also promised me weekends off which meant I could explore the surrounding area. I planned on making the most of that. In September I'd be moving to Wales to start graduate school. This might be the last time I'd have to freely roam in this capacity and I was looking forward to it.

With the other places I'd be forced to socialize, forced to be a part of the community as a whole. I wasn't looking for that. I was looking for peace and for money, that was it. I didn't want to be friendly, didn't want to get involved with anyone or anything. I simply wanted to do my job and go home at the end of a long day without having to think about it.

As luck would have it, despite the fact it had taken several months to secure this job and be offered the other two, on my way through Maryland I'd received a phone call from the director of a summer camp in Massachusetts. She was offering me a job based on my resume, no interview required. The camp was close to Boston and I was bummed not to be able to accept it. I'd made a commitment to this resort, of course, and felt obligated to follow through with it.

My mother cried when I left, the same way she did when I departed for college seven years before. We'd spent the past several months together, just the two of us; she wasn't ready to let me go. She, too, must have felt that this was the ending of something. Or the beginning.

The resort staff, who seemed excited at the prospect of hiring me, didn't know it was getting a second-rate version of me. I was a refugee, arriving beaten and worn in more ways than one. Not only was I sick from the allergies and a few other health problems, but I was also sick in the heart. For the past 2 ½ years I'd worked at a job I'd thought I'd loved and with friends I *knew* I'd loved. It had all come to a screeching halt months before, though, over things I couldn't even think about now. I'd let myself get too caught up in the job, in the things that were going on. I'd meant to take it on as a part-time gig, a way to save money so that I could move to Nashville in a year. Instead, I'd become entrenched with the position and all it entailed.

I quit my job and, worst, I'd lost my supervisor who was also one of my best friends. Even though some of it was my fault and I could accept responsibility for it, I was still in mourning, fearing I'd lost something I'd never truly be able to replace. Coming to the realization that my place wasn't there or with the people I cared about was a knife in my soul. I was scared, nervous about the future, and heartsick; I had to get out of Kentucky that summer.

It took me two days to pack and a week to drive to New Hampshire. I could've made it there faster, but I made several stops along the way: West Virginia, Pennsylvania, Rhode Island, southern New Hampshire...I got out when the scenery suited me and stared at mountains, valleys, lakes, and the ocean. I took pictures of flowers; wandered around thrift shops and outlet malls; sat in the middle of Gettysburg, without a single soul around, as the sun faded behind the monuments; and ate meals in restaurants alone with a book propped up in front of me to discourage conversation.

And I cried myself to sleep almost every night.

I was ready for the new chapter in my life to start in Wales. Indeed, I was excited about *that* part. It was a future I could almost see in my mind's eye; it offered hope, possibility, and adventure. I was *not* prepared for this limbo period in between. I didn't know what to do with myself.

In fact, I didn't know what to do with myself period. In college I was a star student. Not only did I make excellent grades, I'd been a part of several important research teams and had even presented data for bigwigs in Washington D.C. A former teacher proudly described me as "someone bound for the West Wing." I worked full-time, took a full course load, and graduated with two degrees. I felt ready to take on the world, yet I had no idea how to proceed. Life seemed to keep getting in the way. I was technically an adult, but I didn't know how to see the forest for the trees, didn't know how to move forward. I didn't even know what I wanted.

I'd floundered since graduation and hadn't had a real purpose or direction. For a while I'd even been unemployable; not even the stores in the local mall had wanted to hire me. They said I was "too experienced" or "too educated." When I got hired at a local nonprofit I felt a huge sense of relief. There, I could earn a paycheck and bide my time until I figured out my next move. Only life got in the way again and that next move never manifested. The years flew by.

And now, here I was, twenty-five years old, without any real friends or career and I didn't know what I was doing. Depressed, angry with myself, disappointed, and frustrated I applied for graduate school, got accepted, and fled.

I hoped the summer job in New Hampshire would fill a void for me until I could get to Wales and start improving the rest of my life.

△ △ △

The farmhouse that served as the main office/administration building materialized before me, stoic and gleaming white in the dirty fog that looked to be growing denser around me. It rested on a clearing void of trees and undergrowth, the nakedness making it look larger, more imposing than it was. It had three stories, or two full stories and an attic, and black shutters with peeling paint. A line of white-washed rocking chairs grazed the front porch and were turned away from me, looking off into the distance. They were in a little row, perfectly lined up like guards. Without a breeze, none of them moved. Mountains surrounded the clearing in all directions, their brown peaks not yet lush with the summer leaves that would come later. I couldn't see the driveway from the gravel parking lot and even in the clearing I felt a little closed-in. The chill in the air made me glad I'd packed a sweater.

There were only four other cars. The resort wasn't open yet. None of the support staff had arrived. Only the administrative staff were working as my supervisor had explained on the phone. The nearest town was miles away. I'd driven through Malden on the way to the resort. It boasted a store and post office.

Later, there would be kitchen staff, lots of maintenance workers, an entire building of housekeepers, and even counselors to plan activities for the children. The more than five hundred acres would be alive with laughter, footsteps, activity. Now, it was almost deathly quiet and still. Despite the chill, there was no breeze to shake the tree branches or move the impenetrable fog. It was stagnant.

From the porch I could see a large body of water off in the distance. It glimmered in sunlight I couldn't see and lapped against a muddy shoreline. It was called a "pond" on the map, but it was big, more like a lake.

When I walked through the front door I was met by a fresh faced woman who appeared to be in her early fifties. She had short, curly auburn hair and a smattering of freckles across her nose. While I stood in the entrance, trying to get my bearings, she cocked her head to the side and studied me. She didn't offer to rise from the desk in which she was seated. "May I help you?" she asked, neither pleasantly nor unkindly.

"I'm sorry," I said in a rush, "I'm Rebecca. I came a day early. I just wanted to come and say hello and make sure I could find the place. I'm staying in a hotel tonight..."

I waited for some kind of greeting or even a happy acknowledgement but didn't get one. Instead, she continued to look perplexed.

"Oh, I see," she said at last, tapping her fingers on her desk. It appeared what used to be the living room of the farm house had been turned into a front office. The hardwood floors and old radiators were still in place and I felt like I was intruding on someone's home. "Well, I'm Janet. And we weren't expecting you until tomorrow. But I guess since you're here *now* it's okay..."

It was silly, but her reaction made me want to cry. I'd come so far and now there I was, feeling as though I was inconveniencing them (or at least *her*) with my presence. She was my supervisor and had seemed excited about my coming. On the phone she'd been affable, enthusiastic. There was nothing of that now. Not even a handshake. Didn't they want me? It was not a good first impression for me.

"I wasn't planning on hanging around," I tried again, determined to show her I wasn't going to be a problem. "I just wanted to make sure I found the place. I got a hotel room about thirty minutes from here, in Hampstead? So I'll just go on there."

I took like I was making for the door when she laughed. It wasn't a reassuring laugh, but it was friendlier than the look she'd been giving me. "Oh no, it's okay. I was just surprised to see you. Here, I'll introduce you."

Feeling a slim wave of relief wash over me, I let her lead me around the house. There were a few other women working, all of them full-time employees. Most were middle-aged, although there was one young woman named Kory who appeared to be a year or so younger than me. Janet didn't tell me what she did. I tried out my best smile on her, hoping we could be friends. I'd need one there.

After Janet made the introductions I decided to take another leap and satisfy my curiosity, since I was there and all.

"Could you maybe point out where I'll be living while I'm here?" I asked. "I was just curious. And will I be living with anyone?"

"Oh, sure," she said. "I can take you. You'll be sleeping here in the house."

"In the house" turned out to be the attic. The narrow staircase was dark and steep and had a sharp turn that had me wondering how I'd get my small refrigerator up there, but I figured I'd worry about that later. The room was a pretty good size and had a nice view of the pond. It boasted a narrow bed, nightstand, small table, chest of drawers, and rack to hang my clothes on. There was nothing stylish about it, it was actually a little drab and sad looking and had a layer of dust over everything, but I had things with me that could spruce it up. It was cold, but she promised they'd bring me up a portable heater when I returned.

"Now, your bathroom with your shower is downstairs next to the photocopier," she explained.

That's going to be awkward, I thought to myself. I'd just have to make sure I was up, showered, and dressed before everyone got there in the morning. But at least I wouldn't have to worry about being late for work...

As Janet walked me back out to my car I turned and looked up at the farm house again. My bedroom windows looked like two eyes peering down at me, framed by their dark shutter-eyebrows. They were darker than the other windows in the house, as though they really *might* be seeing something.

"Janet, where are the others staying?" I asked as I got into the car.

"What others?"

"The other staff. If I'm up there, starting tomorrow, where will other people be sleeping?"

Janet laughed. "Oh, well, for the next month you'll be the only one living here. Everyone else goes home at 5:00 pm."

Road to the resort

Getting Settled

I t didn't take long to get settled into the room. Janet was even a little warmer and sociable once I returned. Maybe she just didn't take changes in schedules well.

I didn't have a closet, but I had a clothes rack and hung as much of my stuff on the rack as possible by hanging as many things on one hanger as I could. I'd brought "work" clothes for the office (khaki shorts, button-up shirts, jeans, long dresses) but I'd also brought nice summer clothes for the trips I planned to take on the weekends. To help lighten things up my mother took me shopping at Wal-Mart before I left home and bought me a hot pink bedspread, hot pink and purple throw pillows, and a pink shag carpet. Once I got these unpacked and covered the chest of drawers with framed pictures of my mom and grandmother there was a world of difference. I finished things off by tacking postcards to the wall in place of framed pictures. The old attic was looking homey in no time.

Hot pink comforter and pink shag floor rug

In "town" I found the small store offered a few grocery items and there I bought homemade bread, cheese, and fruit. The house didn't have a kitchen, but it did have a microwave and I had my small, dorm-sized refrigerator. The resort kitchen wasn't open yet so I was on my own for the time being. I was fine with that. I planned on exploring the area just as soon as I could. I hoped to find some area restaurants. I had saved a little bit of money and brought it with me, but it would be a few weeks before my first payday and I'd need to budget wisely. Not only did I need to get through the summer, I'd also need to save money to take to Wales with me.

I made sure to call my mother after I got settled. She wasn't pleased about the living arrangements. "You're up there by yourself?" she asked.

I wasn't too thrilled about that either. "I guess so. I didn't know I would be. I knew it wasn't open yet, but I had no idea I'd be in the house alone, much less on the grounds."

"Just keep your phone on you and lock the doors," she warned. I didn't have the heart to tell her the problem with those things yet.

The job itself was easy. I mostly filed documents, answered telephones, and looked up things on the internet for people. Or at least, that's what I was *supposed* to be doing. In the job I'd just left I'd been an administrative assistant for a very busy nonprofit organization and before that I was the transportation director for a summer camp, responsible for organizing the transportation for thousands of children. For the entire first week of the job at the resort Janet and another woman in the office named Lucy spent almost their entire time training me on how to properly answer the telephone. It was irritating.

"When you answer, make sure you speak slowly and enunciate your words clearly," Janet ordered.

"And try to smile when you say hello; they can hear it in your voice," Lucy added.

"I think I've got it now, ladies," I tried to joke.

"Oh, we take our responsibilities *very* seriously," Janet said. "Our voice is often the first introduction anyone has to us so we have to sound professional."

I wasn't sure if she was accusing me of not sounding professional or just assuming I didn't know how to act it. Either way, they continued to "train" me on how to turn the computer off and on, how to photocopy documents, and (no joke) how to use the three-hole punch. I'd organized charity events in the past, given senators tours around our university, worked in the office of some of the highest administrators in town. Yet there, at the resort, they were training me on the right way to collate papers.

I tried to take it in stride, figuring that at least it was an easy job; I could sit back and relax all summer and enjoy my time in New England before the pressures of grad school set in. And this was just the beginning, after all. They didn't know me and what I was capable of. Things would get better and they'd give me more opportunities as the summer wore on. But the feisty side of me wanted to rebel. Two months ago I was planning events and running correspondence to board members; now I was being trained on what a search engine was.

Unfortunately, the weather wasn't quite what I'd expected it to be. The fog never really let up. It stayed cold and cloudy the entire first week. And then there was the heat, or lack thereof. The farm house just couldn't get warm at night. I walked around in long pants and a sweater and sometimes my bathrobe over that after everyone went home. I even drove in to Hampstead (not its real name) and purchased fleece-lined jeans from an LL Bean store. Even with my flannel pajamas, space heater, and comforter my attic bedroom was a veritable freezer. I couldn't tell where the draft was coming from but the cold air filled the room and found even the smallest openings in my fabric, chilling me to the bone. During the daylight hours it was fine; people even complained about it being hot downstairs. At night, however, I huddled in my bed, my laptop in my lap, trying to take my mind off the cold and dampness that slicked my skin.

During the day, the house was filled with busy noises as the telephones rang, the fax machine sputtered, doors slammed, and people chattered with one another. It was a beehive of activity. But after the last person drove off down the hill, it became quiet. I was left standing in the middle of the room, alone, without a thing to do with myself.

I tried to explore the grounds but the terrain around the pond was thick with mud and there were lots of insects that bit me and left huge welts on my skin. No amount of bug spray could keep them away. I spent more time slapping at them and waving them off then I did enjoying the view. As the wind whipped through my hair and the bugs flew around my face and mud seeped into my boots. It just didn't feel worth the effort. The weather seemed to change down there, but there was something more than the bugs that made me uncomfortable. Something besides the mosquitoes pricked at my skin and I couldn't put my finger on what it was. The first time I walked away I felt eyes on my back. The second time I visited I heard laughter that sounded so close I was sure someone was standing behind me. When nobody turned out to be there I chalked it up to an echo, someone on the other side with a traveling voice. I didn't go back down there much after that, though.

Still, the first week went by without much of a hitch. I hadn't found my groove yet, or really made friends (Kory was friendly but distant), but I was trying. It would get better, I told myself. It would get better.

△ △ △

The second week started off alright. I was cold and still feeling slightly uncomfortable with being isolated up there by myself, but nothing bad had happened. I didn't feel scared; not yet. That would come soon enough.

Janet and the general manager, Linda, continued to distrust me with the phones and most documents (although Lucy had backed off) so I didn't have a lot to do, but they didn't seem to mind if I kept myself busy doing other things. I tried to make myself *look* busy and found that if I had Word open on the computer they were generally happy. I don't know what they thought I was doing, but they didn't complain. I used my empty hours working on a novel I was trying to finish writing and composing long emails to my mother.

The living arrangements were a little strange and the advantage of living so close to my job soon wore off any luster it had offered. I had an awkward encounter on Tuesday morning when I came out of the shower wrapped in my towel and found a middle-aged man making a photocopy. Unfortunately, my day started an hour later than everyone else's which meant I could sleep in a little later. I quickly learned this did not mean I could shower later–I'd have to do it the night before or get up extra early and miss my chance to sleep in. I couldn't go wandering around in front of everyone in my robe.

I also learned that my cell phone didn't get service anywhere on the grounds. The whole place was a dead zone. I had to drive all the way into Falcon, a town half an hour away, before it got a signal. Even that might have been okay, except for the fact that I was unable to call out on the office phone in the evenings since once everyone left they turned the phones off and routed them to another site. My mother could call me if we set up an arranged time so that I could get to the phone quickly but basically, the only access I had to the outside world, at least communication-wise, after 5:00 pm was through the internet.

This made me nervous. What would I do if there was an accident?

A beautiful little lakeside town called Falcon became my best friend. It wasn't big but I discovered an excellent inexpensive restaurant there, a tavern or pub really. I had dinner there twice that second week and with the same server both times she got to know me. I took my laptop and worked on my novel while I waited for my food and it was nice chatting with someone who was friendly and talkative. Janet, I discovered, really wasn't sociable -at least not with me. She talked enough to everyone else.

Plus, I liked dining amongst the other people and having folks around. Evenings at the farm house were lonely and isolating. I mostly spent my off hours huddled in my bed, reading, or working on the computer. There wasn't a television, although I picked up a small, cheap one at Wal-Mart hoping I could pull in some basic channels. I couldn't. I thought about going somewhere and buying some craft supplies, but I didn't really have the money to spend. I was looking forward to the rest of the staff coming in so that I'd have other people to talk to.

Fortunately, I had internet access back at the house. I spent hours online in the evenings, the faint glow of the computer screen reflecting on my pale face while the darkness tugged at me outside my window. My mother and I sent long emails to each other and I used my time to research the area and find things to do. But I spent so much time on the computer during the day that by the time evening rolled around I was usually ready for a break.

△ △ △

It was at the end of my second week that things started to get a little troubling. On Thursday, I was downstairs on the computer, researching youth hostels in Boston. It was late, around 10:00 pm, and quiet. The farm house was almost always quiet. The sound of my own breathing was usually the only thing I could hear, especially when I was downstairs. In my own room I kept the radio and CD player on a lot.

Suddenly, a loud thump clamored above me. It was louder than a sound an animal could have made, and I was almost sure a large piece of furniture had given way and tumbled over. Worried I might have inadvertently caused something to tip earlier, I jumped up and took off towards the sound of the noise. Scrambling up the stairs, I made it up to the second floor and took a look around. It was dark, but the two small office rooms were flooded with light as soon as I flipped the switch. The illumination was a stark contrast to the blackness and I shielded my eyes for a moment, letting them adjust. Nothing was out of place. There were two other rooms on that level, but they were locked. I just had to trust everything was okay in them since I couldn't look.

Next, up the long, narrow staircase I went to my bedroom. Even from the doorway I could tell my room was untouched, too. My books were all on my nightstand, stacked up neatly, the chest of drawers was pushed up against the wall as it should be, and my clothing rack was still bolted into the wood, all the clothing still in place.

The noise had no source. It had simply been a clatter, probably something on the roof like a large tree branch blowing around, and I was scaring myself because I was there all alone and it was usually so quiet. At least that's what I told myself.

Trying to laugh it off, I went back downstairs to the bathroom on the second floor. It was probably time to turn in for the night anyway. While I was washing my face and getting ready for bed, however, I heard it again. The sound was thunderous, actually shaking the walls of the small room around me. There was no mistaking it for a wayward tree branch. I placed my washcloth on the sink and stepped outside the bathroom, straining my ears. What was it? My heart started racing as visions of a burglar entered my mind. I was alone, helpless. Nobody would even find me until morning. I made a move to run up the stairs and collect my car keys when another noise sounded– footsteps and they were directly above me.

There were only two rooms on the third floor–mine and a storage room. It just had a bunch of boxes. I tried to keep that door closed because I could see into it from my bed and I didn't like looking into another dark room, especially since the boxes cast odd shadows. But the door continued to be reopened. I assumed people kept going up there to get things they needed.

The footsteps paced back and forth above me, lightly, hesitantly. I could feel slow, icy dread creeping up my spine and down my arms, chilling my fingers. Someone was up there. And maybe even more disturbingly, they'd been there for a long time. It was hours since everyone left the house. The idea that I'd been in the house, supposedly alone, all evening and someone else had been hiding terrified me. There was no way I could outrun anyone, even with the narrow staircase slowing them down. My best bet was to try to scare *them*.

Stepping out into the lounge where the copier was I raised my voice, "Hello!" I tried to make myself sound brave, forceful. The noises stopped. I waited for as long as I could, holding my breath to see if I could hear anything else, but it was quiet. "I'm not alone here. There are two maintenance workers downstairs and I have my revolver on me." My declaration and thin voice sounded funny even to me.

Nothing, not a peep. I stood there for what seemed like forever, just waiting and listening. The floorboards up there were very creaky but if someone was really there they weren't even shifting their weight. All was still in the house. I began talking myself out of what I'd heard; I was paranoid, delusional, overreacting. It was a mouse, a rat even, or a raccoon that had sneaked through the walls. I was being silly.

With trepidation, but newfound courage, I walked back up the stairs, a three-hole punch from a nearby desk in my hand, and looked in my room. There was nothing there. The small room across the hall from me was dark, the door open. I flipped on the corridor light and peeked into it. It was empty as well.

I got very little sleep that night.

$$\triangle \ \triangle \ \triangle$$

The next morning, I approached Janet with what had happened the night before. I wasn't one to let anything go. "Janet," I started lightly. After all, I didn't want her to think I was nuts. "I heard a really loud noise last night and what sounded like someone walking back and forth in that empty room in the attic. Has anyone else who's lived here ever heard anything...weird?"

"What do you mean?" she asked with a bright, sunny smile that didn't quite reach her eyes.

I briefly explained what I'd heard the night before and how I'd been scared it was someone breaking in on me.

"No," she replied with a slight shrug. "Nobody else has ever heard anything before. And lots of people have stayed here in this house. Could have been the wind, or an animal. Or maybe you're just special and sensitive and can hear things others can't."

Yay me, I thought to myself as I took a seat at my desk. But, it was Friday and although I hadn't planned on going away, now I was thinking it might be a good idea.

My money was scarce, but it was payday and I knew how to do things on a tight budget. I'd once backpacked Eastern Europe on $16 a day. Since I'd already done some research I knew where I wanted to go: Concord, Massachusetts. I'd always wanted to see the Louisa May Alcott house and while I was there I could also see the Old Manse, visit Walden Pond, and kind of make a literary trip out of it. I found a hostel in nearby Harvard and booked two nights in it. Ecstatic at the idea of getting away and going someplace I'd always wanted to visit, I felt lighter in step than I had in a long time.

"You look happy," one of the women said to me as I passed her in the hallway. I couldn't remember her name.

"It's Friday!" I exclaimed with a laugh. "And I'm going away for the weekend."

On my lunch break I packed my suitcase and printed off directions from Mapquest. I also got some CDs ready for the drive which would take a few hours. When Janet came back from lunch she'd already heard about my plans and sounded excited for me. "You'll love it there," she gushed, showing genuine enthusiasm. "I've been several times and it's a beautiful town. So much history!"

An upset stomach held me back longer than I'd anticipated. Everyone else was already gone by the time I loaded up the car to leave. I was about ready to pull out of the driveway when I remembered the CDs. I ran back up to my room to grab them and as I stood in the room, placing them in a bag, I heard the soft sound of footsteps as the climbed up the narrow wooden staircase outside my room.

"Hello!" I called out. I thought everyone had left, but maybe not. Maybe Janet had come back to check on me. "Who's there?"

Nobody answered. The footsteps stopped as soon as I opened my mouth.

Feeling a little bit of anxiety now, I walked to the staircase and peeped down, but the stairwell was empty. My car was the only one in the parking lot.

It was a good weekend to get away after all, I decided.

Danvers

Getting away for the weekend was a balm for the spirit. The hostel I stayed in was a lovely farm house located on a real working organic farm and I slept like a baby under a handmade quilt. The rest of the hostel was full of school kids on a weekend trip and the sounds of their running back and forth down the halls, laughing, and staying up until the wee hours of the night comforted me. It was the best sleep I'd had in two weeks–maybe longer.

I played tourist in Concord and after seeing the historical sites, went to the movies and watched a silly Jennifer Lopez film as a treat. Away from the resort the air was clear, the temperature warm, and the skies bright and sunny. As I stood outside on my second evening and gazed up at the night sky it occurred to me that it was the first time in almost two weeks I'd been able to see the stars; the fog at the resort crept in early and didn't dissipate until late the next morning. I had no idea how much I'd missed the stars, the moon, and even fluffy white clouds until I saw them again.

I never minded traveling alone; indeed, I often found myself going on trips by myself. I didn't mind my own company and I never really felt alone; being around other travelers and tourists, eating next to people in restaurants, and even sleeping within proximity to others in hotels and hostels...I enjoyed it and felt a part of something. But being up there in the farm house at the resort, surrounded by fog and cold and people who I couldn't even tell if they wanted me around or not? That was lonesome. I was beginning to feel locked up inside my own head–not a place I particularly wanted to be.

I was still recovering from what had happened back in Kentucky and had hoped this job would be the fix for that. So far, it was making me feel sadder. That job, at first, had merely been a stopover point for me while I figured out what I wanted to do with the rest of my life. But I had fallen in love with the children I worked with and formed close bonds with my co-workers, especially my supervisor who became almost like a sister to me. We'd eaten lunch together almost every day, celebrated birthdays and holidays together, and even gone on vacation to Ireland where we'd laughed over wine and taken silly pictures of one another at ancient ruins.

And then I'd been sexually harassed by someone there I trusted. More than just frightening me, it had hurt my feelings. Embarrassed me. My somewhat stable world had slipped out from underneath me and I felt myself floating, drifting. If I could go back and erase it all and pretend it had never happened, I would have. But that was impossible.

I wasn't making friends, mostly because there weren't any people around yet, and I was just spending way too much time by myself. When I took the job, I hadn't realized I'd be alone so much. Over the phone, Janet had told me that "lots" of staff would be living at the resort along with me–hundreds, even. She had left out the part about them not arriving until weeks later.

But getting away was nice.

In Concord I went on a guided tour of the "Little Women" house and bought my mom souvenirs. I sat on a rock at The Old Manse and meditated in the stillness around me. I visited Walden Pond and bought a small booklet of Emerson's poetry which I read over a bowl of steaming vegetable soup at a tavern. Surrounding by the quaintness of the small town, the laughter of the tourists, and the feeling of being amidst the memories of some of the greatest writers I'd ever known, I somehow felt safe.

I checked out of my hostel feeling a little wistful; the weekend just wasn't long enough. On the drive back to New Hampshire I took my time, stopping off in Salem to tour the House of the Seven Gables, and I caught myself as I passed a sign for Danvers. As an avid horror movie fan, I loved "Session 9" and had watched it multiple times. I couldn't contain my excitement. I knew it was filmed on location at the old mental hospital in Danvers and that the hospital was abandoned and empty. The urban explorer in me couldn't get over my good luck of being so close. I also knew the security was fairly tight and that my chances of getting in were not good.

Still, I couldn't be *that* close and not check it out.

It didn't take me long to find the mental hospital. I just stopped at a gas station and asked. Without even looking up at me the attendant had rattled off the directions by heart, probably used to giving them out to eager explorers such as myself–people who had more enthusiasm than sense.

The hospital was still abandoned. I belonged to several urban explorer groups and had done my research on the hospital. As an urban explorer, I always thought people like me were probably a couple of principles short of criminals, with only our intentions setting us apart. I loved finding old buildings (houses, churches, factories, etc.) that had been abandoned.

When I could get permission, I got it. In most cases, however, the known owners of such structures were obscure. In those instances, I was known to shimmy through windows, doors, or whatever openings I could find. Intrigued with history and architecture, I went armed with cameras, long pants, and flashlights. Like others, I documented my findings for others to look and speculate over. I didn't touch anything or bother it. If I got hurt, I didn't sue. I was just fascinated by neglected beauty and looking for an adventure.

Many an urban explorer had aimed for Danvers–the Holy Grail of horror movie loving, ghost hunting, urbexes. Some had made it and reported back to the others, their digital pictures pored over jealously. I had waited my turn for some time. I knew that it was difficult to get through to, thanks to increased security. I also knew that with the dwindling daylight, I wouldn't have much time to find an opening and make my way in. Many things scared me, but exploring old places for whatever reason didn't.

Still, I was no fool. Even I knew better than to creep around an abandoned mental hospital in the Boston area, alone, after dark. The spirits that might be lurking there didn't necessarily scare me but those who might be using the place for less altruistic reasons did. There were stories of mental patients who, used to their former sanctuary and unable to deal with the outside world, broke back into the only home they'd ever known. I'd heard tales of satanic groups using such places for their rituals and offerings, although I suspected those were just that–tales. With the light security, there was also the risk of vagrants setting up shop, a dilapidated mental hospital offering more shelter than the streets at night and providing a modicum of comfort with the large rooms and insulation.

I also watched quite a few crime shows so the threat of serial killers in dark corners never fully left my mind. Still, I'd come that far...

The hospital sets on a hill, overlooking what was once probably farmland. It's hidden from the main road below and there were no signs pointing the way as I wound up the broken road. Of course, there were other signs: No Trespassing, Keep Away, Stay Out, etc. We urbexes tended to take these as a challenge.

The light was pale and thin. There wouldn't be a sunset that evening so the waning daylight was simply fading out instead of declaring its goodbye with a colorful bang. Everything was gray and colorless: the sky, the air, even the trees. I held my breath as I took my time up the hillside, half waiting for a security vehicle to come run me off, half excited as I watched for a sign of the famous Kirkbride Building.

Suddenly, through the trees, I caught the color of red brick peeping through the branches. Then more, and then more.

As I turned the corner, there it was before me, towering in the sky like a majestic, glorious castle. Barely watching where I was going, I pulled in front of it and came to a dead halt. With its turret-like towers, multitude of windows, and wings that spanned the acreage like a giant bat, it resembled a palace more than a hospital. Indeed, despite its boarded-up windows, cracked sidewalks, and the ragged weeds that poked up through the asphalt it was one of the most stunningly gorgeous pieces of architecture I had ever seen.

30

I turned off the engine and quietly opened my door and got out, camera already booting up. Despite the busy road below me, it was deathly quiet up there on the hill. The sky was beginning to darken, and a chill filled the air, the breeze ruffling my hair. I skirted the edge of the building, snapping pictures as I went, and headed first to the abandoned cemetery. The headstones were difficult to see due to the undergrowth, but they were there, some decrepit and pocked and others crumbling and on their sides like dominoes.

I was totally alone. I knew that others found their way up there almost every day and I half expected to meet another explorer, but there was no doubt I had the place to myself. The air was tomblike; still, I think I could have heard the hitch of a breath on the other side of the complex.

Up there in the snowy whiteness of the fog I felt cut off from the world, much like I did back at the farm house. I could no longer see the road below me or hear the whirr of the car engines as they raced by. I couldn't even see through the grove of trees that peppered the hillside. It was just me and the lonely old buildings, despondent and abandoned.

Picking up my pace, I turned and went back to the Kirkbride building. There was no possible way for the movie to have depicted the grandness or even the sheer size of it. It took me more than twenty minutes just to skirt the perimeter, all the while snapping my camera in anticipation. The windows were boarded up tightly, like eyes closed against the world. If there was anything inside, it didn't see out.

I knew how to get in. I was *going* to get in! Soon, I found the hidden entrance. Not hesitating, I pushed the board aside and stepped in. With the closed windows, I expected it to be pitch black inside, and it was. Standing still to collect my bearings, I waited. Above me, the sounds of mice scurrying across the floors and larger animals thumping against forgotten doors filled the air. The outside might have been still, but the interior was alive.

Momentarily, my eyes adjusted to the light that seeped in around the boards. It was pale, but I could see the hallway, strewn with papers and garbage. This was not the rubbish of people like myself, but what had been left behind from the hospital's closing.

Using the flashlight on my cell phone, I illuminated my way. Mindful not to be disrespectful and step on anything important, I walked to the first door and peered in. It was an office, a desk pushed haphazardly in the middle of the floor. A chair was turned on its end. I tried taking a picture, but it was too dark.

The stillness was palpitating. I could almost taste it. There had once been activity in this building - everyday sounds that echoed down the halls and filtered through the rooms the same way the shadows did now. Now, the silence was oppressive. It was so soundless, in fact, that there was almost movement within it; deafening movement that caused the blood to rush to my ears.

It was unusually warm inside, especially considering how chilly it was outside. I took my jacket off, feeling beads of sweat on my forehead. Back in the hallway, the air was thicker, closing in. I felt as though I was chest-deep in water, unable to catch my breath properly. Taking small gulps of the stale air, I turned to try the next door when a creak that was so loud it sounded like it was opening the door to another universe stopped me. It could have been three feet away from me or on the other side of the building-the sound in there was deceiving and the acoustics played tricks on my mind. In fact, my own footsteps seemed to be a beat behind, echoing long after I stopped walking, like my shadow was having trouble keeping up.

I was no longer alone.

There were no footsteps, no further creaks, no other noises; but I knew without a doubt that someone or *something* was aware of my presence and taking note of it.

Turning, I headed back to the entrance in which I had shimmied in through. The feeling of a thousand eyes was on me and invisible fingers clawed at my back, rustling my shirt and pulling at the strands of my hair. Light fingers trailed down the backs of my arms, touched my thighs through my jeans. The darkness was thick, almost tangible. Through it, I moved in slow motion as though in a dream. Nothing about being there felt real. Maybe it *wasn't* real, I thought peacefully as I closed in on my exit. Maybe I was still in my car, leaving Salem, sipping on my Pepsi and listening to Allison Moorer on my CD player. Or maybe I'd never left Kentucky at all and was still asleep in my bed, an old episode of "Designing Women" playing in the background.

Once outside, I headed to my car. The air there was only slightly better, fresher but still thick. The pressure on my chest eased up a bit but the cold fingers still danced on my neck, on my arms and legs. The sun was down and gone.

Inside, I locked the car doors and started pulling away. I was promptly stopped by the quick burst of a police siren and the flashing of lights. I'd been caught. The cruiser came rolling up to a stop alongside of me and the officer, heavyset man with a thin moustache, stepped out and walked over to me. As I rolled down my window, he admonished me. "Ma'am, you don't want to be up here," he chided.

"Just taking a few pictures," I smiled, showing him my camera.

"I'm up here every day, and this place stays with you. You know what I mean? I wouldn't be here unless you had to be." He shivered for effect and then offered me a light smile.

Terrified now that I might be arrested, I put on my best face and explained that I'd taken my pictures and wouldn't be back. He appeared more bored than upset by my appearance however, and simply waved me on back down the hill.

I left him without getting into any real trouble and headed down the potholed driveway. Again, I drove without hurry, the red towers looming behind me. This time, although the windows were still boarded up, it felt as though the eyes were open.

A few miles outside Danvers, the sky broke and the strongest thunderstorm I had seen in years struck. Bolts of lightning slashed through the sky like swords while the rain pounded my car in bullets, forcing me to pull over into a rest area across the New Hampshire line. As I sat there in the darkness, my doors locked, the world seemed to fall apart around me as nature fought against itself and those foolish enough to be out in it. Unable to see more than a few inches from the car, I waited while the wind and rain rocked the vehicle back and forth, the noise earsplitting.

When it finally lifted, it came to an abrupt stop without any warning. One minute it was storming, the next it wasn't.

I drove the rest of the way home in a fog so thick I was unable to see the end of my car. I might have left Danvers, but I had the distinct feeling that Danvers had not left me.

Week 3

T he next week went by in a painful blur. Monday morning and afternoon went by without a hitch but in the middle of the night I had to go to the bathroom and a few steps down from the bottom I slipped and fell down the stairs, hitting the back of my head hard on the wood. I wasn't sure why I slipped. One second I was walking towards the door at the bottom, the next I was seeing stars. It jarred me then and left me feeling a little woozy, but the pounding headache I developed an hour later lasted for days. It made it difficult to sleep, eat, and focus on what I was doing. It also left me in a foul mood.

"Do you need to go lie down?" Janet asked me with concern after I snapped at Lucy for something inane.

It was Thursday. I hadn't slept well all week. The headache made it difficult to fall asleep to begin with, but that wasn't the only problem. Whenever I'd drift off I'd hear noises. They weren't loud, and I wasn't even completely sure they weren't in my head, but they were bothersome enough that they kept me awake.

Sometimes the sounds would be outside my room, just there by the door. They were small, scratching sounds at first and later developed into vocalizations; whispers that filled the dark and pressed in on me but without real clarity. Other times they'd be in the stairwell, just faint rumblings of padded footsteps, as though someone might be trying to quietly fade away without being heard. Still unconvinced they weren't part of the house or even small animals in the walls, I wasn't scared, yet, but I found myself listening for them more and more. They started when it got dark, after everyone left.

"I think so," I said. "I'm sorry but this headache is killing me. I've tried taking everything in the world for it but nothing is touching it."

With everyone else still in the farm house, working, sleep was easier. I didn't have any trouble falling asleep and staying there. Just knowing that others were below me, going on with their lives, and that their bodies were near was enough to make me feel safe. This sleep was dreamless, effortless. When I woke up, though, it was dark, and I was disoriented. I didn't fall back asleep until well into the middle of the night and by then I could only sleep for a few hours before I had to get up for work again. That sleep was full of obscure dreams, distorted images, and bolts and starts. Images of my childhood friend, David, plagued me. I hadn't thought of him in a long time. It was restless. Sometimes I'd wake up to the sound of the noises outside my room and think I could almost understand what they were but then they'd diminish and I'd be left alone in silence again, frustrated. Maybe I was starting to go crazy.

I still wasn't getting the responsibilities at work I'd hoped to get, either. Although they'd finally decided I could be trusted to answer the phone, few other duties were passed on to me. Earlier, I'd hoped this would be okay, that it would make the job easy and fun and leave my brain open for other things. It wasn't fun, though. It made the work day long and boring. I couldn't just sit there in the office and goof off because there were too many people in and out, but neither did I have anything to keep me busy.

If anything, it made me even more depressed. I wasn't being used for anything. My education and whatever intelligence or talent I had was being completely wasted. Maybe I didn't have any talents or skills at all, I'd think bitterly to myself. I tried not to delve into self-pity, but it was hard, especially when I didn't have anything else to do. The mind is a terrible thing to get lost in sometimes.

Without any extra money to go away that weekend I decided to stick around and explore the local area. The rest of Thursday and Friday passed in a blur with my head still hurting made worse by the incessant chill and fog that never wanted to let up. I didn't feel well enough to get out and drive anywhere. Friday night found me sitting in my room, the CD player on, and Nanci Griffith singing about "The Speed of the Sound of Loneliness." At least that was the *only* sound I heard and none of the other, strange noises I'd been hearing all week.

Feeling sorry for myself as I sat there on my bed, trying to read and eating my supper of a sourdough roll and slice of cheese, I gave in to some self-pity and let myself have a good cry. I cried for the friend I'd lost at my old job, for Dolly my cat I'd had to leave behind at home, for the future I wasn't sure of, for the friends I didn't seem to have, for this sudden inability to sleep I'd developed, for this awful pain I was having, and for the loneliness I was experiencing. I even cried because the season finale of "Lost" was getting ready to air and I didn't have a way of watching it. I just cried for it all.

I cried through three songs. By the time the fourth one came on, I was aware of the noises right outside my bedroom door. Maybe the music had been too loud before or maybe, with my tears, I hadn't been giving them my full attention. But now I could hear them without any trouble. Not quite footsteps, they brushed back and forth, like a woman in a long, heavy gown that was dragging the floor. I slowly reached over and turned the music down and the sounds grew louder. Something definitely seemed to be pacing near my door. As I listened, I noticed an almost rhythm to the noise. It would grow louder, louder, *louder* and then fade, fade, *fade*—as though it might be walking away. I realized with a start that it was going back and forth not in front of my door but from my door to the room across the hall.

I don't want to hear this now, I thought, *I just don't*.

Now, feeling scared AND sorry for myself, I turned the CD back to "The Speed of the Sound of Loneliness" and turned the volume up. The sounds outside my door immediately stopped.

Confused, I turned the music down again. The sounds picked back up. When I resumed the volume, it stopped. With the music playing, yet still kind of low, I approached my bedroom door with caution. I couldn't hear anything on the other side of it. Placing my ear as close to the door as I dared, I held my breath and waited. Nothing. I returned to the CD player and stopped the song. Halfway across the floor to the door, the "swishing" was so loud and fierce the door rattled in the process. "Shit!" I shrieked and jumped straight up into the air.

Skipping back to my nightstand, I turned the music back on, this time as loud as I could stand it. It's not like anyone else was around to hear.

Interesting, I thought, as I dried my eyes and blew my nose. *I have a ghost and they must be lonely too.*

△ △ △

The next morning I woke up, ready to take on the day. I popped some Excedrin Migraine and hopped in the car. There were covered bridges to see, White Mountains to explore, and, well, whatever else was in New Hampshire for me to find. I was there to see and do things, right? I couldn't let a little headache and ghost keep me cooped up in the house all weekend.

I spent all day driving through the White Mountains, exploring towns like North Conway with its outlet stores and Laconia where I got ice cream and sat outside and enjoyed the sunshine.

RDP 2005

Just getting out of the house again for an extended period, and not just for supper, helped. I was amazed at how different even the air was away from the resort. Once the car climbed out of the tunnel of trees and entered the valley below, the fog lifted, and the sky was blue again. It was easier to breathe and even what was left of my headache cleared away.

Being gone gave me plenty of time to think. My old childhood friend, David, had been on my mind since the dream I'd had and I told myself I'd write him when I got back to the resort. The last I'd heard from him was a year ago or more when he'd sent out a mass email and said he was getting married. I'd lost touch with a lot of people in my life and now, trying to figure out my next move, I was anxious to form some connections. If I couldn't make new ones, maybe I could reestablish old ones.

The way my brain worked, I was afraid I might forget writing him at all, so I used my phone to access my email when I finished my ice cream. It would only let me type a few lines in one message so I sent him a brief one: "You married yet?" and hit "send." We'd known each other since I was seven. He'd seemed happy the last time I'd talked to him.

It felt good to get out and reconnect with someone from my past, even though by the end of the day I hadn't heard back from him yet. I drove back to the resort with a lighter heart. Just being in the sunshine made me feel a little better.

△ △ △

Sleep did not come easy that night. The headache returned almost as soon as I entered the house.

Maybe it's mold or dust or something in here, I thought as I made my way up the dark staircase, wishing I'd left a light on. It was an old house, after all, and I'd been there three weeks and had yet to see a real good cleaning. I'd been left to clean my attic room myself upon arrival and had to make do with soap and water and an ancient vacuum that did little but shake the dust around.

Still rationalizing what was going on around me, I tried to put on a brave face and settle in. I needed the money, after all, couldn't stand the thought of having to go home with my tail between my legs, and was an adult. I had handled worst in the past–surely I could handle some ghosts. After all, I'd never really heard of a ghost hurting anyone. It was really just a problem of mind over matter, right?

Without much else to do, I closed myself in for the night and tried reading. The noises began almost immediately.

They started softly at first, light enough they might have been a tree branch scraping the side of the house (had there been any trees around it) or a bat flapping its wings against a window. A "creak" here, a light "thump" there; they were mostly sounds an old house makes while it's settling. Those I could ignore. I tuned them out, turned my music on, and focused on "The Mists of Avalon."

But they only grew louder. Now, the thumps that had emanated from downstairs earlier were outside my door, soft sounds that could have been someone bumping into a wall or catching their foot on the stairs. And the creaks became rhythmic, someone walking back and forth or up and down the stairs. They were purposeful sounds, made with intention and not the result of some old pipe or groaning rafter. A footstep, a handclap, a whistle...these were noises I know and recognized.

I kept reading, trying to immerse myself in the book. If I could just get lost on the aisle of Avalon and find myself with Morgaine and Lancelot I could forget what was going on around me, what sensed me and knew I was there.

Ghosts can't hurt you, ghosts can't hurt you...I repeated it over and over again, my body growing colder and heart racing with every new thud against my door, every pounding on the stairs.

Maybe they couldn't hurt you, but they terrified me.

I tossed and turned that night as the sounds outside my room grew increasingly louder and louder. The footsteps continued up and down the staircase until the wee hours of the morning in an almost comical fashion, like someone was having trouble remembering what they'd come for. I was too afraid to open my bedroom door and peer outside.

At least my room was bright, safe. Nothing had happened in there. Sleeping in the dark was not an option. I soon found that I couldn't sleep with my back to the center of the room, either. Although I hadn't seen or heard anything directly in my bedroom, I couldn't risk making myself that vulnerable and slept with one eye open. As a result, I got very little sleep and woke up on Sunday feeling cranky and exhausted.

I'd planned on another day of exploring, but it was impossible. Instead, I hung around the farm house and tried to write. The room was starting to feel like a prison to me by afternoon. The four walls offered nothing to new to look at and even though my windows offered a beautiful view of the pond and mountains, everything felt so far away from me.

Still nervous about opening the door, I hadn't even left the room it to go to the bathroom. I finally passed out from exhaustion in the middle of the day with the radio on and got several hours of sleep before waking up at sunset, only to face the night sounds again.

Even I appreciated the irony of the fact that I could explore a place like Danvers yet have trouble with a few creepy noises outside my room. But every day the darkness of the woods surrounding the resort seemed to crush in on me a little harder and the gravel road to the farm house seemed a little longer. If I could just hold out until the other staff members arrived, I'd be fine.

I kept repeating that to myself.

I'd be fine.

David

David wrote me back the next week. Having put my foot in my mouth, I'd asked him the one question that was a sore spot with him—if he was married yet. Apparently, both the wedding and relationship were called off and it was fairly recent. I felt bad for asking, but it had been such a long time since we'd talked I didn't know there was any trouble there.

Still, it was nice to hear from him. Finally, I had someone to write to. Other than my mother, that is. I'd struck out with making friends of my fellow co-workers. We barely had more than a friendly, casual relationship in the office. Some days they'd pass right by all day and do scarcely more than glance my way. One day I went an entire day without speaking to anyone other than those who called in on the phone— the ones I could get to before Janet jumped in and answered, that is. I'd tried inviting Kory to dinner in town but struck out there. The other women were all married with families and despite my hope that one would invite me over to dinner one night for a home cooked meal, it never happened. No matter what I did, I felt like I was inconveniencing people. If I asked Janet a question, for instance, she'd look up with an exasperated look on her face and bark, "What?" The main manager didn't interact with me at all and often looked at me as though trying to remember who I was and how I got there. They didn't need me to work in the office. I was starting to wonder why I was there myself. Ironically, I was starting to feel like a ghost myself, just moving through the rooms, keeping to myself, and trying not to interrupt the things around me.

Writing to David gave me the opportunity to at least prove I still existed. Between him, my mother, and the waitress at the tavern over in Falcon, I had regular communication with people now who knew who I was and expressed interest in what I was doing. The waitress, whose name I'd learned was Grace, was slowly becoming my closest friend—a thought that might have depressed me under normal circumstances but now seemed okay. She was probably a year younger than me and always greeted me with a warm, welcoming smile. On her breaks she'd sometimes slide in across from me at my booth and we'd chat about the town, current movies, and plans for the summer. The restaurant was a busy one, and she always appeared to be the only one working, but she was never too busy to throw a few kind words my way and I lapped them up like a hungry dog.

And then there was David.

There are some people in your life you can go years without talking to and then pick right back up where you left off. We were like that. We'd bonded as children in our weirdness (he ate bugs and talked to himself and pretended a unicorn picked me up every night and took me to a magical land under Lake Michigan) and although as adults we had little in common something just kept us hanging on. Maybe it was nothing more than a shared past, but it was enough.

Now, during the day when Janet didn't give me anything to do and I was sitting at my desk, bored senseless after cleaning it for the fifteenth time that day, I could write David long emails. At first, he might go a day without answering them. Soon, however, he was responding almost immediately. I think he must have been lonely, too. I described the grounds, the house, what was going on at night, what had happened in Kentucky, how sad and lonely I was feeling, and my excitement about graduate school. He wrote about his job, his breakup, and new recipes he was trying out.

Neither one of us got out much.

I didn't know much about David-the-man. We hadn't spoken in a long time and my memories were of him as a little boy, or him as an awkward teenager. In some ways, it was like having a pen pal I'd never met.

On some nights, when it was hard to sleep, if I could get up enough courage to open my bedroom door I'd steal downstairs in the darkness, flip on the low-wattage lamp at my desk, and write him longwinded emails.

Even while the noises above me carried on throughout the wee hours of the morning and terrified me to the point where I often wanted to throw my things in the car (forget the blasted refrigerator-I'd find another one) and hightail it out of there, my letters to him were an anchor of sanity. Writing about the weather, a movie I'd just treated myself to, a nightmare I'd had, a song I'd heard and liked...anything to keep my mind off of what was going on around me.

Usually, after work, I'd drive into town and eat dinner. Sue Ellen, my favorite server at the tavern, was always waiting for me, ready to serve me a bowl of chowder or a burger. Her smile was a welcomed sight after spending a day of mind-numbing work with people who hardly said more than a word to me. I was aching to talk to someone and found I sometimes held her back from her duties by spilling out everything that was on my mind. If she minded, she didn't show it. I didn't tell her about what was going on in the farm house. Part of me was still trying to explain it away in the hopes that it was simply the sounds an old house made; creaks and groans from settling and wind.

But I knew it wasn't.

Instead of being a "problem child" for her, I tried to be enthusiastic, bubbly, friendly. Everything that was bottled up inside me just spilled out as soon as I saw her and I couldn't wait to laugh with someone, talk to them.

Now that I was writing to David, I could talk to him as well. The first phone call was a little awkward since we hadn't spoken in a long time, but we started with text messages and worked up from there. Soon, I could spend an hour or more on the phone with him and not even realize the time was going by.

"That's the first time I've laughed in a long time," he said after the first call. We were recovering from different things, but still mending nonetheless.

Sometimes I'd stop and pull over at a gas station or store on my way back and call David. We didn't always have things to say to each other that were of any importance, but he was laughing more at my stupid jokes and that was a chance from the morose tone he'd had when I'd first gotten back in touch with him. I laughed a lot, too–the most I did all day. It was fun talking to him. I liked him more and more as a person and not just someone from my childhood. I also liked the fact that he was a piece of me and my history and in a time when I wasn't real sure who I was or where I was going that was comforting.

He knew about the house, how I felt living there. "I'm spooked and afraid," I told him frankly. "I can't sleep. I'm thinking of buying some Tylenol PM or something."

"Have you tried talking to what's going on?" he asked. "Seeing if you can help it?"

No, I hadn't, but my mother had suggested the same thing.

"I'm afraid it might actually answer back," I joked.

The truth was, the fear in me was starting to become a routine, something I counted on having every night. A very big part of me was now afraid it might be *me* causing what was going on.

The New Staff

W e're getting some new staff today," Janet announced with as much excitement as I'd seen her show.

I'd perceived something in the air by the way everyone was running around the downstairs, shuffling papers and cleaning up more than usual. The news lifted my spirits as well, although I felt incredibly tired. What little sleep I was getting I achieved in spurts–a few hours here and there while it was daylight and then a restless tossing and turning at night. The radio helped but if the song became too fast, too loud, or was even something I loved I'd wake up in an instant. I also woke up every time I turned over, snored, or felt any changes in the air currents.

It was getting old.

"How many are coming?" I asked. They'd put me to work filing that morning and I welcomed the chance to do something different. Keeping busy made the day go by much faster.

"Five today," Tina (I wasn't sure what she did, but I thought she was pretty high up on the totem pole) answered. "And then a few more on Friday. We're starting to fill up."

"Are they kitchen workers?" I asked hopefully. I was losing money quickly by the amount I had to eat out. Meals were worked into my salary but since the kitchen wasn't open yet, I was on my own. Barely earning more than minimum wage, my paycheck didn't stretch far.

"No," Janet explained, "these are interns so they'll be living in the intern cabin down by the pond."

My heart sank. No food yet. And the intern cabin was pretty far from the farm house–a fifteen-minute walk or short car drive. While there would at least be other people on the grounds and I wouldn't be completely alone anymore, they'd be so far away it would still feel like it. And they'd all be living together which meant they'd probably bond right away. But I was determined not to let that stop me from being friendly and trying to do my best to make a good impression. This was my first real opportunity to make friends and I was going to grab it. (Hopefully, without looking desperate.)

The new staff members rolled in around lunchtime. There were five of them, as promised, and they were all college students studying various things from park management to health sciences and education. From the easy way they talked and joked with one another it appeared they'd known each other before their arrival.

"They've been getting together all year for retreats and workshops," Janet explained as we sat down for lunch in the cafeteria. It was my first day of getting to eat onsite.

Apparently, from here on out, the kitchen would be open for lunch. That still meant I had dinner on my own, but it was something.

"Hi," I said to everyone, trying to appear cheerful and friendly as I sat down at the long table with them. "I'm glad to have some company here!"

The others introduced themselves and then went back to talking to one another, laughing at some inside joke. *Well*, I figured, *I'd get to know them eventually.* There were three girls and two guys. The oldest guy, Trent, was a graduate student. He was tall and lanky with a goatee and scar above his right cheek.

Jeff, the shorter and better looking of the two, looked like a west coast surfer with his curly blond hair and tan skin. He looked like he'd just stepped out of a LL Bean catalog with his leather hiking boots, khaki shorts, and flannel shirt.

Sherry, a chunky brunette, had a sweet smile and big green eyes. She occasionally caught mine and smiled at me. Julie, a smaller girl with bony arms and legs played with her hair a lot and rolled her eyes whether she was annoyed or found something funny.

Then there was Maya, another grad student, from Wisconsin. Maya appeared to be dating Trent. Tall, like him, she was extremely athletic looking and had a loud, booming voice.

I spent the remainder of the lunch period talking to Janet. I apparently had a roommate coming in four weeks. This was news to me, but not necessarily not bad news. Surely I'd be able to sleep then. I was a little surprised that I was only just now learning about a new person and knew I'd have to move some of my stuff around, but I didn't really care. The more the merrier.

"I hope this isn't a problem for you," Janet said, enunciating every word so that they were crisp and tart.

"Oh, no," I replied with a smile. "I think it will be fun. What will she be doing here?"

"She'll work in the office with you and help you out. You'll share your workload."

It was all I could do to keep from laughing aloud at that. *Share my workload?* I didn't do anything! Now I was suspicious, though. Did they know they were going to hire her or were they displeased with me and thought another set of hands was needed? It was true I spent most of my time biding time, but it was because they wouldn't give me any responsibilities!

△ △ △

At the end of the day I overheard the new staff talking about having a movie night in their cabin. I hoped they'd invite me, but they didn't. It was on the tip of my tongue to ask if I could join but since not one of them even looked my way, much less suggest it, I stayed quiet. Too shy to invite myself over, I simply said goodnight to everyone and watched as they all filed out and went their separate ways. The farm house was, once again, quiet and lonely.

I spent the evening lying in bed, starting on a new book ("The Book of Ruth") and listening to an Iris Dement CD. The house was unusually quiet that night. Somewhere there on the grounds there were five people hanging out together, laughing and watching some kind of movie. I wanted to be with them. Several times I got up and started to drive over to their cabin but then talked myself out of it. I didn't want to be pushy. Or appear too desperate.

Still, knowing they were nearby made me feel lighter and I slept better. Nothing bothered me.

The next day, I caught them at lunch talking about a new movie that had just come out. "Why don't we go over to Portland and watch it?" Julie, rosy cheeked and soft spoken, asked. They were kind of grouped around my desk so I pretended I was part of the conversation, even though they hadn't included me in the slightest.

"I'd like to see it," I said. Actually, I had no idea what it was about, but I wasn't going to pass up the opportunity to get out with others.

The five of them turned, almost in unison, and gazed down at me. Some of them wore surprised looks on their faces, like they'd forgotten I was there.

"Well, we can't all fit in Julie's car," Jeff countered. "We'd have to take two."

"I don't mind driving," I volunteered. "My car's pretty big. I could take half."

So, that evening I found myself chauffeuring around a group of interns as we made a long trek to Portland to watch a movie I really had no desire to see (looking on IMBD had been a bad idea).

Still, once we were there and sitting in the dark auditorium and laughing together at the silly parts I felt calm and at ease. I was sort of making friends and while I hadn't clicked with anyone yet, they all seemed pretty friendly. And at least I was putting myself out there and trying. That had to count for something. Nobody offered to buy my ticket, help me pay for gas, or even say thank you when we got back, but I tried not to let that bother me.

I was exhausted from the drive and knew I'd probably fall asleep as soon as my head hit the pillow. As I crawled into bed, though, the sounds started up almost immediately. First came the long, slow footsteps up the stairwell. Then, the shuffling outside my room.

I was wide awake now, sitting up in the bed, staring at the door. My lamp cast a soft, warm glow but its light didn't extend far. Most of the room was bathed in a dark, murky shadow. My breath hitched as I clutched the covers up to my chin and twisted my fingers, popping the knuckles one by one. A night of reprieve had almost made me forget how scared I could get; perhaps the mind could forget fear the way the body could forget pain.

Usually, the noises stopped outside my room. Nothing had actually come inside. But now, as I watched in horror, my doorknob began turning. It was just a slight movement at first, so slight I almost missed it. Initially I thought it was a shadow on the brass knob making it appear to move. But then the creak of the old latch gave it away and I jumped to my feet. I was halfway across the floor when the door inched open about half a foot and stopped.

"Hello?" I said into the quiet room. "Is anyone there?"

There was a stillness that was almost more intense than the noises had been. I couldn't hear anything but my own breathing and it echoed in my ears, filling my head with the sound a large seashell might make if you put it up against your ear.

Trembling, and with my blood running an icy river through me, I took another cautious step forward, my hand outstretched to slam the door closed just as soon as I had the gumption. I didn't know whether to take my chance and run out the door and down the stairs or pull the shelf in front of it and barricade myself in.

With a deliberateness that nearly made my heart stop, the door suddenly slammed shut, causing me to jump back at least a foot and trip on my pink shag rug and land on the floor.

I waited for an instant to see if anything else would happen and when it didn't I began walking towards the door again, this time determined to close it as hard as I could and set something heavy in front of it. Maybe it was one of the interns, thinking it would be funny to play a trick on me? Or someone had come in downstairs and caused a draft to blow up and open it? I didn't think so, but I hoped it was true.

Now, just a few feet from the door, I watched again in horror as the knob turned with ease and the door once again inched open almost half a foot before slamming shut with a firmness that made a few of the pictures I'd taped to the walls flutter to the floor.

Tears sprung to my eyes and I moaned a little then. The idea of bursting through the door and into the darkness of the landing was almost as frightening as imagining what could be on the other side of my door, waiting for me to emerge.

Out of the corner of my eye I saw my camera on the small chest of drawers and I raced over and picked it up. Turning it to the video setting, I aimed it at the door. Maybe it just wanted attention; maybe it wanted to be known. At any rate, I was going to get proof of what was going on. Within seconds, the knob was turning once again and the camera picked up every movement as it inched open and slammed shut. I continued videotaping as it did it a second time for the camera, then I turned it off.

We were quiet, the door and I, as though both of us were waiting for the other to make a move. "I'm not afraid," I said suddenly. "You can't hurt me and you won't."

Finally, having had enough, I opened the door myself.

In utter darkness, I tried to peer into the empty room across from me and down the stairwell but couldn't see a thing. "Please leave me alone," I whispered. "Go away. You're scaring me."

Nothing answered back.

When I closed the door for the last time I put a chair in front of it, just in case.

△ △ △

"Janet?" I turned my chair around to face her, dreading the conversation I was about to have. As usual, she looked perturbed by my voice. She was busy writing something on her desk and barely glanced up at me.

"Yes?" she responded in a clipped tone.

"Remember when I asked you if anyone staying here ever heard or saw anything?"

"Uh huh, I remember." She looked up now and peered at me through her wire-rimmed glasses that made her appear older than she was. "Why?"

"I've been hearing things again," I answered trying not to sound as crazy as I felt. "Actually, I hear things almost every night."

"What kind of 'things?'"

I shrugged. "Lots of different things. Sometimes it's footsteps, sometimes whispers, sometimes thuds. It comes from different places in the house, depending on where I am, but it's loudest right outside my bedroom door."

Janet appeared pensive as she studied me closely. "It could be animals, something in the walls. We found a raccoon in one of the attic walls not too long ago. It hissed something awful. Made a racket."

"I thought about animals, birds and mice," I admitted. "But I don't think that's what this is."

"You think the house is haunted?" she pressed lightly, going back to her work. I could tell she was finished with the conversation.

"Yes, I do," I replied firmly. "Is there anywhere else I can stay? Like maybe with the other interns? At least until my roommate gets here."

"No, I'm sorry. We actually like to keep the interns separate from everyone else. We encourage them to bond, develop teamwork amongst them. They're meant to learn as a unit and an outside influence might upset that. Do you understand?"

No, I didn't. I thought it sounded weird.

"What about another room? A guest room maybe?"

"Our season starts in just four weeks," she answered, obviously frustrated with the conversation. "We are really trying to get everything organized and opened. We just don't have time to put you somewhere else and then take you back out."

I didn't see what the big deal was, but Janet clearly wasn't open to working with me on this or discussing it any further. I turned around and went back to my "work," entering data into the computer that really took all of five minutes, but I was trying to stretch it out. But the more I thought about it, the madder I got. First, they had me up there alone without any means of communication with the outside world, other than the internet. (Which came and went, depending on the weather.) It was a big house and only the back door locked. The front was always open. I didn't have a key. There was no way to really protect myself in there. And now she wouldn't even entertain the idea of me staying somewhere else on the property, despite the fact that I was upset.

An hour later, Kory came into the room. I'd been given another set of data to enter and was busy with it. She, who hardly ever spoke a word to me, stopped and peered over my shoulder. "You're still doing that?" she asked accusingly. "I would've thought you'd been a lot faster. Isn't this what you did at your old job?"

"I *am* fast at it," I snapped back. "This is a new set."

Raising her eyebrows, she stomped away but I could hear her complaining to the director, Linda, about how "rude" I'd been to her when she was "just asking a simple question." I continued to seethe.

That evening I pulled my laptop out and tried to work at the small table in my bedroom. It was still a little light out but would be dark soon. I'd wanted to go into town for supper but didn't have any money. Instead, I made do with a bowl of cereal and piece of bread.

The house was quiet, but I wasn't surprised. Things usually didn't get started until a lot later. Right now, it was just the normal sounds of an old house settling. Those sounds I could deal with. They might make me jump from time to time, but they were "normal." I could differentiate them from the others.

I'd left my bedroom door open on my last trip up and the room across the hall was closed. I was still aware of it, though, and knowing there was a direct line between it and me at my table made me nervous. I was having trouble concentrating and kept looking up, expecting to see something in my doorway.

Shaking my head at my silliness, I finally got up and walked over the door. I'd never get anything done if I didn't close it. As I placed my hand on my own door, however, the one across the hall slowly slid open, like a gust of wind might have caught it.

Curiously, I watched as a thin, pale shadow of light appeared in the opening of the empty room. It wasn't enough to be an overhead light, or even a lamp, but it illuminated the room enough that I could see some of the boxes. The door wavered for a moment and then, just as slowly as it had opened, closed to again. I could see the light peeking out under the door and casting rays on the hardwood floor in front of it. Then it simply went out, leaving the hallway in darkness again.

△ △ △

Two nights later I was taking a shower after returning from supper and after wrapping myself up in my robe, I was halfway up the stairs when I heard an unmistakable bang from the empty room.

That alone made me jump, clamoring for the handrail as I nearly lost my footing and went flying down the wooden stairs. But the noise was followed by a long, weary sigh that reached right down into my soul and turned and twisted it until I found myself leaning back against the wall, tears forming in my eyes. The sigh was lonesome, pensive, drained. Whoever or whatever had made it was exhausted, beyond sad. Just tired.

In my own frustration, I began to cry. I couldn't help it. Naked, wet, without anyone to talk to or go to, I felt like I was slowly going insane and was as defenseless as a person could be. They were just noises, I thought to myself, why can't I live with them? Noises couldn't hurt me. But the sigh had been so human, so sad and desperate. It sounded the way I felt.

Resorting to an old childhood trick of combatting fears of the dark, I turned to music. In a voice as loud as I could, through my tears I began singing the first song that popped into my mind – "The Speed of the Sound of Loneliness." It just seemed to fit.

The shuffling in the upstairs started and became more pronounced as it neared the top of the stairs, but shutting it out I let my voice grow louder and louder as I closed my eyes and held onto the rail. I couldn't see around the corner at the top of the stairs, but my overhead light was on in my bedroom and this made the landing glow. Opening my eyes, I peeked upwards and nearly lost my voice as I saw a tall shadow poised in the landing, standing as still as I was.

Neither one of us offered to move and I didn't know what to do. Slowly, still singing, I began moving up the stairs. As I did so, the shadow faded away, moving as deliberately as I was. The door to the empty room closed with a thud. When I reached the landing, nothing was there. By the time I was finished I'd sung the song three times and the house was quiet.

I popped a CD into the player, turned the volume up, and lay down. For awhile, at least, everything was still.

Salem

You've been awfully quiet," Janet remarked. It was Thursday afternoon and everyone was getting ready to pack up for the day. "Everything okay?"

"Just a headache," I answered. and I wasn't stretching the truth. I had a horrible headache and stomachache, too. Everything felt a little "off."

"Well, if you're *ill*, maybe you'd better go lie down," Janet said sharply. Her words were nice, but her tone was cryptic and stringent. Perhaps I was feeling too sensitive. but I felt a little bit like the problem child who was being a burden on everyone.

"I'm fine," I shrugged. "I'm thinking I might go to Boston for the weekend. Get a change of scenery."

"That's a good idea," she replied absently as she thumbed through a file. "Better go while you can, before everyone gets here."

I started to ask her what she meant but decided not to. Still, her words bothered me. One of the reasons I'd taken the job was because she'd told me in my interview that I would have the weekends off and could travel. I was working for a travel review site and posted my reviews online; writing reviews was how I made most of my extra spending money. I needed to be able to continue that throughout the summer.

One of the big reasons I'd turned down the other jobs was because I was expected to join in all the activities and participate with few days off throughout the week. I knew a lot of people liked that about summer jobs, and that's why they applied to summer camps, but that wasn't what I was looking for and I'd been clear about that from the beginning: I was simply looking for a summer live-in position that would allow me the flexibility to move around and join in when I wanted to.

But maybe she hadn't meant anything by it.

△ △ △

Friday afternoon rolled around and I made my way to Boston. I have to admit, my step was lighter as I walked out the door and said goodbye to everyone. In fact, I all but danced out the door. After all, I was on my way to my favorite city in the United States and would be spending three nights there since Monday was a holiday.

The time away was just what I needed. I did a little sightseeing, a little shopping, and ate some great meals. Being in a big city alone didn't bother me since there were so many people around at all times. I made friends with a girl from Hong Kong who was staying in my hostel room and we even drove down to Newport, Rhode Island for the day and looked around the mansions and beautiful seaside town.

On Sunday night, several of the girls in my hostel gathered in the common room to talk about their weekend. I was reading but still felt included. We'd all had dinner together and gone out for drinks afterwards. Now, everyone was tired and trying to relax. One of the girls had whipped out her curling iron and was working on my hair. Two others were doing each other's nails. An Irish girl sat in the middle of the floor on a ratty rug, reading us Hollywood gossip from a tabloid. It was the first time I'd been included in a group, and actually felt included, in a long time. I needed to travel more. I'd forgotten just how much I enjoyed it and liked the camaraderie it provided.

When they brought up Salem I joined in their conversation. I'd only been once, and that was to go to the House of the Seven Gables, but I kept meaning to go back and explore. After several hours of talking, laughing, and drinking a few glasses of wine with the girls I began telling them about my summer home and job.

"I just can't wait until my roommate gets there," I finished at last. "I think the being alone is the worst part of all."

"Just one question," a Polish girl from Warsaw asked in impeccable English. "Why are you still there? Why don't you just leave?"

The others nodded their heads in agreement.

"That's a very good question," I answered. "And I don't have a single *good* reason. Money, mostly. I need it to live on and to take with me for grad school in the fall."

"Aren't you terrified?" a Chinese girl asked with wide eyes. "How do you sleep?"

"I don't," I laughed. "I've slept better here than I have in weeks." And that was the truth.

"It sounds scary as hell," Jenny, an American with jet black hair and two nose rings, snorted. "And it doesn't just sound like a regular ghost, man. This thing, whatever it is, sounds like it KNOWS you. You know what I mean? It communicates with you."

"Well, I've never talked to it and had it answer back," I interjected.

"Doesn't matter," she shook her head. "You sing or play that music, it stops. It can hear you. So it's not just one of those leftover energy shits. This thing has feelings, has a brain. You'd better be careful; it might not be a ghost at all."

Telling these strangers about my nights in the farmhouse did make it sound scarier and more terrible. It was as if the distance in miles gave me an emotional distance with more clarity. Suddenly, I felt stupid for continuing to stay.

"They're just noises though, right?" I posed this question to Vickie, my roommate, once we were back in our room. "That's what I keep telling myself. I mean, it's not like I'm seeing ghosts or a lady in white or anything. Just sounds really."

"Maybe," she said slowly. "But even with 'just noises' it's obviously bothering you. I don't think any one person can say, 'That haunting is not so bad.' It's how it affects YOU that matters the most. And if you can't learn to live with them then you don't need to be there. Honestly, I don't see why you would stay if you're not happy anyway. Just the way you describe the job would be enough for me to say my goodbyes and quit."

"I don't like the job," I admitted. "I feel lonely, sad. Afraid in the house, but sad in the job. Maybe if I enjoyed the job I could deal with what was going on in the house, you know? Like it would even it out a little."

△ △ △

I was feeling much more like myself on Monday afternoon when I checked out and started back to New Hampshire. With extra time I pulled into Salem and did a little more sightseeing. I was charmed by the town itself, and even with its cheesiness and tourist traps it was a quaint place with easily navigable streets and shops and I enjoyed myself there. There were loads of shops selling crystals, charms, and books on witchcraft and after walking past a few and window shopping I decided to go in one.

The shop was empty except for the manager, a middle-aged woman in a black shirt and long blue skirt. She had a necklace with a fairy pendant on and sat on a stool behind the desk reading a Sherlock Holmes novel. I approached her cautiously, having taken in all the crystals and herbs, and asked for her help the best I could. I tried not to feel silly. After all, this was a store that sold books like "Reincarnation for Beginners" and crystal balls. Once I was finished explaining my situation, she laid down her book and took a long look at me, her eyes searching.

"Let me ask you something," she said at last.

"Yes?"

"Have you seen or heard anything in your room?"

"Well," I replied, "I hear most things in my room, but sometimes I'm downstairs. And the shadow on the landing was right outside my door."

"No," she shook her head, "I mean have you actually *heard* anything that is *originating* within your room?"

"No, I haven't. It seems to stop before it gets that far. It plays with my door, stops outside my door. It's never come in, though."

"Well," she tapped her fingers on the counter and tilted her head thoughtfully. "That's a little unusual but not implausible. If you hear the noises in the rest of the house but not in your room, and yet the spirit is obviously trying to come *in* your room, then I'd say you already have something keeping it out. Do you know what that may be?"

"Huh?"

"A talisman, dear. A protector. There's something in your room that is protecting you. What could it be? Because that would be helpful to know."

I honestly had no clue. "I don't have anything with me like that. I was hoping you could *give* me something," I said with a nervous laugh.

"I can help," she said with seriousness, "but you've already got some of the most powerful antidote with you. It is something protecting you: a talisman, a good luck charm, a picture, a letter..."

I thought about the things I'd packed and brought from home with me but nothing was very sentimental, just clothes and makeup and books. Except, of course, for my pictures. "I have a picture of my grandmother on the wall," I said. "She died when I was seven. Could that be it?"

"Yes, it's very possible. Somehow her spirit is reaching out for you and holding the other one back. Has she appeared to you before and done this? Protected you from something?"

I nodded. When I was a child we'd lived in a haunted house for four months. My mother and I thought we were going crazy. Not long after we moved in, I'd come down with a terrible illness. A friend was staying with me and had woken me up from a feverish dream with a scream. She claimed to have seen the ghost of my grandmother sitting on the bed beside me. My fever broke later that afternoon and I became well again, as if nothing had happened.

"She has," I answered. "Only once, but I think it was important."

Again, she looked at me with those deep eyes, as though measuring me or reading my mind. Maybe both. "You feel things, don't you?" she finally asked. Her tone was gentle. She had such kind eyes and a gentle voice I wanted to cry. I felt like she was reaching out to me, seriously trying to help.

"Sometimes," I said carefully.

"Not just ghosts, spirits, things like that. You feel things from people."

I shrugged. "I'm no psychic. I can't read minds."

"But you can read feelings. You know when someone is sad when they act happy to the world. You know when someone doesn't like you but pretends to. You know when someone is looking at you with disdain, being disrespectful even though their words and body language says differently. You can read people."

Yes, that was true. I'd always read people well. Even as a child I'd disliked those everyone else wanted to fawn over, just because of a feeling I got. Sometimes, it was hard for me to make friends because I felt their true character emanating within moments of meeting someone and after that it was just too difficult to give them the benefit of the doubt.

"Yes," I whispered.

"You're a sensitive, child. You hurt deeply. You feel things deeply. You try to cover this up by being alone, by acting confident, even by lying. But you carry a hurt in you for the world. This thing, and I don't know what it is, it feels that. It's drawn to you. And it won't be the last. I'm quite sure it wasn't the first."

"Why?"

"I don't know. Maybe it trusts you. Maybe you're motherly to it. It's seeking comfort and your energy is providing some. But it's also draining you. You're pale, you're weak, you're disheartened. It will feed off this and more. You must be careful."

Elsa sent me home with several black candles, two crystals, and sage to burn in all the corners. She also recommended I get some salt and make a line around my room, added protection to keep it from crossing over. The last thing she gave me, this item for free, was a book of candle spells. "Your energy," she said confidentially as two young women dressed as Goths entered the store, "is being wasted. You have power and you don't know it. White magick, the only real magick, is for you. Honor what's inside of you. Train it. Cultivate it. It will make you stronger in mind and heart."

△ △ △

It started raining on the drive back and once I crossed over the New Hampshire line the drops were so large I could barely see. I pulled over into the rest area, much like I had on my last trip, and waited it out. In the meantime, I called David and talked to him.

"I'm scared," I admitted. "I bought sage today and black candles and a white candle and some gemstones, but I'm still scared. I don't want to go back." I found I was crying into the phone and it mortified me. The last thing he probably wanted to deal with was a crazy, emotional woman.

"I know you don't," he said softly. "And I don't like the idea of you being there alone. It doesn't matter what anyone else thinks; there's something there and it's targeting you. You can't live like that. I don't think I'd be able to."

"I never thought I'd be this scared," I sniveled. "You have no idea how much I don't want to go back, how much I just want to leave everything and get on the interstate and start driving. The idea of pulling up to the house, getting out, walking up those stairs...I don't know that I can do it!"

He let me cry for several minutes and the two of us sat there in darkness together, both on opposite ends of the country but feeling close.

"I can't leave," I said after the tears had slowed down. "I'm such a failure. I made a mess out of my last job. I'm making a mess out of this one. I haven't made friends, my boss doesn't like me, I'm miserable. I wanted this to work, I really did! I can't go home. I can't go home and face the fact that I can't keep a job."

"But you weren't fired from your last one," he pointed out. "You quit. And it was the best thing to do. Anyone would've done it."

"Oh, I'd have been fired eventually," I said darkly. "I just quit before they could do it. It's ME, David, me."

"Maybe it's too soon. Maybe you shouldn't have worked so soon after what happened. You went up there feeling fragile, feeling emotional. You were already in a state."

"You think I'm just hearing things that aren't there? Like some kind of manifestation of my thoughts and emotions?"

"No, no," he said hurriedly. "I just mean that maybe...maybe it came out because you were a little weak."

I sniffed again, new tears starting to form. Everything felt like my fault.

"I wish I could come up there," he said at last. "I'd like to visit. I've never been to New Hampshire. It's someplace I've always wanted to go." I knew this was his way of saying he'd like to see me.

"I wish you could, too," I said. "I wish someone else could hear and see these things. I feel terrible to be reacting like this but I just don't know what to do. And you could also see my fabulous butt. Over the last year I've gained ten pounds and now I have a rear end to be proud of." We both laughed and the mood was lightened.

David didn't treat me like I was crazy or overreacting; he believed me. So did my mother.

"Just come on home," she advised. "Don't stay there if you don't want to."

"I can't, Mom, I have to stay. I need the money."

"I'll give you some," she all but pleaded. "We'll figure something out. Just come back home for the rest of the summer. We can spend more time together before you leave."

But as I turned out of the rest area and started on the long drive back, I thought more about my reasons for staying. It was true I needed the money. I'd spent my savings (little as they were) just by driving up there and the taking care of little things my first couple of weeks. I had nothing to take with me to Wales other than the student loans I'd be getting.

But it was more than just the money. I'd made a commitment to work the job, I'd told everyone back home I was leaving, and I'd emotionally prepared myself to leave for the summer and start on my next adventure. *This* was my adventure. I couldn't turn back now. Grad school didn't start until the middle of September. I'd applied for tons of jobs back home and been turned down for everything, despite my pretty good resume and degree. I couldn't just admit defeat and go home with my tail between my legs and kill time for the next three and a half months. To go home now would like giving up, like saying I couldn't hack it. I'd already left one job recently because of the conditions; I couldn't do it to another.

I would tough it out. I would be okay.

The rain stopped but, once again, the fog set in. This time, though, it was horrendous. The fog was so thick on the road I slowed down to an excruciating 45 mph and then to an even slower 30 mph until I felt as though I was creeping along the asphalt. As the only car, it was dark and lonely and I couldn't see beyond my hood. I crept along at a turtle's speed, watching the white line along the shoulder to reveal curves to me. If not for the line, I wouldn't have known when to veer my car to the right or left. It was my saving grace. The fog swirled and dipped and cast shadows on the car and in the air. It even seemed to creep inside the air vents and claw at my face and neck as the coolness sent chills up and down my arms and legs. What should have been a two-hour drive at most took nearly four. By the time the farm house came into view I was shaking, cold, wet, and tired.

The house was dark, a giant shadow against the dense, thick air. There weren't any lights on and my window peered down at me from the night sky, a sentinel. Any other time I would've found the house beautiful, inviting. I loved farm houses. I dreamed of living in one someday. But this one...this one was a nightmare.

I put my hand on my door handle and made to get out, but found myself rooted to the seat. I couldn't do it. I just couldn't do it. I was physically unable to get out of the car. The thought of going into that house and spending the night in its viscosity, enclosed by its clamors, was too much. I could feel the bile rising up my throat and threatening to come out with a might. I forced it back down, gagging on its bitterness. In frustration, I laid my head on the steering wheel and cried. I was a loser, a baby, an insane woman who couldn't even manage to walk up a flight of stairs and deal with a few thuds and what in all likelihood could be animals trapped in the walls. I beat myself up for several minutes while the tears flowed. I wanted David, I wanted my mother. I wanted to sleep through the damn night. Then, without another thought, I pulled myself together, turned the car around and drove to the other side where the interns were living.

A light was still on and the two guys were up watching television. "I'm sorry," I apologized as they led me in. "I just got spooked. It took a long time to drive back tonight from Boston, the fog is awful, and I just can't stay in that house tonight. To tell you the truth, I'm a little spooked because I forgot to leave a light on. Can I sleep on your couch?"

"Sure," Trent shrugged. "No problem."

Jeff brought me his sleeping bag and a pillow and began setting up the couch for me. I felt silly, but not as silly as I thought I would. At least I would be able to sleep.

As Jeff worked, Trent sat down in one of the easy chairs and studied me. Finally, he laughed out loud. "Honestly, from what we've heard, we're shocked you've lasted as long as you have. We've all talked about it."

"What do you mean?" I demanded. Jeff was finished so I slipped my shoes off and perched on the edge of their saggy sofa. It smelled faintly of spilled beer and something sweet I couldn't put my finger on, but I wasn't going to complain.

"I worked here last year as a counselor for the kids. The chick who had your job last summer? She came down here in the middle of the night, her second week, just like you did. I was down here hanging out, playing cards. She looked terrified. Had a baseball bat in her hands. Shaking like crazy she was. Said she couldn't take the noises. Said she wasn't going to go back there again."

I looked at both Trent and Jeff, stunned. Jeff nodded his head in agreement, as though collaborating with Trent's words. "You're serious?"

"Yeah," Jeff said. "Everyone knows that house is haunted. We were just talking about it last night. There's even some kind of weird-ass story they used to tell kids about. About a blind girl who sits in the basement, in a chair, and just stares at the wall."

The guys laughed but I didn't think it was funny.

I was *furious*. I'd asked Janet if anyone had heard anything about the house or had any experiences there and she'd shrugged me off as if I were a fool. And now these guys were acting like everyone was familiar with the ghosts of the farm house, like it was common knowledge weird stuff went on in there.

I didn't believe in the blind girl story, but obviously there was enough action in the house that it had spawned a tale like that. Couldn't she have at least been honest with me?

A Night Visitor

resisted the urge to bring up my newfound information with Janet. I spent the next two nights on the interns' couch, however. They didn't seem to mind me bringing my pajamas and hanging out with them. Although I couldn't read or work on my book or do anything private, at least I had company. I still didn't feel as though we'd made friends with one another yet, but we were getting used to each other and that was something.

"I don't know that I like them," I informed David as I ate supper at the tavern. I took to calling him when I ate sometimes. It made me feel like we were having dinner together. "But at least they're people to hang out with."

"Well, sometimes you need the company," he agreed. "Hey, I looked at flights. Where's the best place for me to fly into? Manchester?"

It was his idea to come and visit me. We'd agreed upon the Summer Solstice, thinking it might be fun to spend this holiday together and do something interesting, like going for a midnight hike.

I was really looking forward to seeing David again. He was now my closest friend, my confidante, and I was depending on him. Over the past few weeks he'd become my lifeline. When I was feeling especially scared or alone I'd reach out to him in my mind, focusing on his voice or a memory or something he'd said to me and like a balm I'd feel almost instantly better. I didn't want to share this with him for fear of scaring him off, but I thought I might even be falling in love with him a little bit. I was rational enough to understand it was probably due to my own seclusion and the fact that I was in need of companionship, but it wasn't a bad feeling.

On the third night, the interns decided to play some drinking games. I wasn't opposed to drinking; in fact, I rather liked alcohol. But it had been awhile since I'd played any kind of alcohol-related games. I mostly liked to do my drinking quietly over a conversation or at a concert.

These guys were hardcore about their recreational drinking, however, and took it very seriously. They brought out balls and cups and all kinds of contraptions and after about half an hour I was feeling sick to my stomach and silly. I might have only been twenty-five, but I was feeling every bit my age and at that time twenty-five felt old.

I couldn't drink as much as they did, or as quickly. I was already feeling like I was going to vomit so Lord only knew what the hangover would be like. Janet was probably about ready to kill me with my constant headaches and stomach problems. I certainly didn't need to exacerbate things and damage our sticky, tenuous relationship.

I could put up with the drinking, though, and excuse myself from the hilarity of the juvenile stunts. When three of the interns brought out the weed, though, I knew it was time to call it quits. Having the alcohol on the resort's property was one thing. I'd thought about bringing in my own bottle of wine or Baileys to help me sleep at night, but marijuana was pushing it.

I didn't want to sound like a goody two-shoes, but I also didn't want to get in trouble, either. I was a long way from home without anyone to bail me out and the last thing I wanted was to get fired or end up in jail. I'd never smoked pot before and the idea didn't appeal to me in the slightest. We were already drunk; how much further from reality did we really need to get?

Besides, the evening was wearing thin and these people didn't feel like real friends. They weren't trying to get to know me and only seemed to be tolerating my presence. The sensitivity Elsa had spoken of rang true. The interns didn't really even like me; they weren't sure why I was there and neither was I. I was a sixth wheel. I tried, it didn't work out.

Ghosts or not, I excused myself from the cabin and decided to brave the farm house again.

The day before, I'd gone into town and picked up some Tylenol PM. I took it now to put myself to sleep. It worked to an extent, I certainly fell asleep fast enough, but it didn't keep me there. The noises almost immediately woke me up.

They were insistent, predatory tonight. The pacing back and forth outside my door was louder, heavier, and even more frantic. The pauses, which usually came after every few steps, were nonexistent. I felt the fear crawling on me, almost strangling me. The effects of the medication heightened my sense of awareness; the drowsiness made me weak.

Trembling and with exhaustion, I finally sat up in bed and said, very sternly, "Please leave me alone. It's been a long night, I'm tired, and I just want to go to sleep."

I'd no sooner laid back down when I heard the faintest of whispers wafting through the walls. They were muted at first but gradually grew louder until I could make out actual words.

"Don't bother her," the first one said. It was toneless, even, neither male nor female.

"Leave her alone," the second one echoed, the sound bouncing off the walls and closing in around me.

"Let her go to sleep..."

Shutting my eyes in panic, I squeezed back some tears and prayed for sleep to come.

△ △ △

Janet took me to lunch the next afternoon. "I'm worried about you," she said. "You don't seem happy."

"The noises are keeping me up at night," I explained. "The ones I told you about? I'm having trouble sleeping. And I guess I'm a little homesick."

For the first time she appeared sympathetic and compassionate. We talked about my mother, being so far away from home, and resort life. I could see the kind of person she was outside the office, outside of the job. Some people were different away from their responsibilities and duties. I knew that; I knew I was.

It made me that much more homesick and sad for Angie, my former supervisor (and more importantly, friend) and our time together. At work Angie had been efficient, serious, and mostly no-nonsense except for the moments when she blasted 80s rock or Pink on the facility's loud speaker before we opened or we took an extended lunch break to discuss the details of Anne Rice's *Sleeping Beauty* series.

Outside of work, though, Angie and I had vacationed together in Ireland and England and had sneaked into crumbling abbeys after closing time, climbed the Tor in an attempt to locate the mystical Avalon, and gotten slightly tipsy at a restaurant overlooking cobblestones in Galway called The River Goddess.

I wanted to tell Janet the truth: that I just couldn't continue to stay in the farm house, that things were too scary for me and that so far the isolation of living there alone and having few people to associate with outside of working hours was taking a huge toll on my mental well-being. But I couldn't. All of those things made me feel pathetic and I was finished with feeling that way. Talking and writing to David was helping me gain my confidence back after having it shattered months before and I was looking forward to a new future, whatever it might be. I couldn't let a few ghosts get in my way.

"I'm worried about how much I'll have to participate in the resort," I admitted at last. "When I took on the job I thought I'd have my weekends off but not too long ago you kind of made it sound like I might not." I hated to rock the boat, but I needed to get that off my chest, at least.

Janet sighed. "Well, we *do* expect you to participate. You will have to eat your meals with us, participate in most of the evening activities, and stay most of the weekends. But most of the staff enjoy those things. You will, too."

I fought the urge to cry. *No,* I wanted to shout, *I won't enjoy those things. I specifically asked you in my interview if I would be required to do them and you told me I wouldn't. And now you're reneging on that.*

But I kept quiet. This lunch, I felt, was her way of trying to do something nice for me. I didn't want it to end in a disaster.

We rode back to the farm house in silence, Janet most certainly feeling better about having treated me to lunch and getting to know me a little more–me feeling more and more trepidation about the job.

△ △ △

On Friday I decided to save my money and not leave for the weekend like I'd originally planned. I'd contacted a hostel in Vermont, but my funds were getting low and I needed to build a bigger nest egg. Instead, I decided to go to the movies.

It was nearly 11:00 pm when I left and the drizzle that was present when I entered the theater had turned into a torrent, creating a heavy fog on the road. I pulled over to a gas station before I knew I'd lose my signal and gave my mom a call to let her know how I was doing and that everything was okay.

"Where are you?" she called through the distance and rain. "I can barely hear you."

"I'm in the car," I shouted back. "I pulled over to call you. It's raining really hard and it's foggy. I'm on my way back."

"Are you okay?"

I sighed. "I think things will be fine. It's just–"

The phone beeped a couple of times and then went dead. I usually got a pretty strong signal where I was but the rain and fog probably threw it out. I waited several minutes and tried to call my mother back but couldn't. Figuring I'd at least made an effort, I drove on, once again taking the roads at a turtle's pace.

This time, I'd remembered to leave lights on inside so that I wasn't returning to a dark building. Still, with the fog swirling around it and the torrential downpour soaking me to the skin it wasn't the most welcoming of sights.

Once inside, I locked the emergency exit and then made my way up to my room. I wanted to take a shower to help warm myself up but I didn't like being in the shower after dark; I felt too vulnerable wet and naked and with no way to get out if someone came in on me. Instead, I wrapped up in a heavy robe and donned my slippers. After making myself a mug of herbal tea downstairs in the microwave I popped two Tylenol PMs and settled into my room with the Nanci Griffith CD playing. It was the only one that kept the worst of the noises at bay.

I was just about finished reading my latest Nora Roberts novel and almost dozing off when a loud noise startled me and caused me to drop the paperback to the floor. This wasn't one of the regular sounds – this was most definitely the sound of someone banging loudly on the front door.

I quickly jumped up and looked out the window, but the parking lot was empty, at least what I could see of it through the rain and blackness.

Figuring it might have been one of the interns, I hurried down the stairs. As I reached the second floor, the pounding on the front door echoed through the house a second time. "I'm coming!" I hollered, as if they could hear me through the thick wood and walls.

When I reached the front office, however, and looked through the front windows, the porch was bare. Still, I unlocked the door and stepped out into the night air. Tugging my robe closer around me I strained my eyes into the night. "Hello! Is anyone there?" I couldn't see much beyond the edge of the porch, thanks to the rain, but I didn't see any movement.

As I stepped back into the house and closed the door, the noise sounded again – this time from the back of the house. Someone was knocking on the back door.

It was almost a straight line from one door to the next so I ran as quickly as I could but when I was within mere feet of the emergency exit, the knocking stopped. Again, a look outside showed me an empty porch.

Now I was alarmed.

I stood there between the two doors in the middle of the house and tried to think of what to do next when the knocking came again at the front. It was so loud and heavy that the very walls around me shook and I could all but feel the hardwood under my feet rattle. A framed document fell off the wall and clattered to the floor, the glass shattering and sending shards everywhere.

There wasn't an intern there who was capable of making such an impact with their fists alone. I didn't know *anyone* who could. Both doors had glass panes in them and my position allowed me to see both of them at once. I couldn't see anyone on either side of them. Sinking down to my bottom, I buried my head in my hands and started to cry. I didn't care how senseless I was or might have appeared or what I should have been doing–all I could think was that someone or something was trying to get inside and kill me. I wanted my mommy.

After giving into the fear for several minutes I got up and tried the phone. It was dead. I couldn't call out anyway but thought I might have at least been able to dial 911. I'd heard you could do that. I tried my cell, too, but didn't have a signal. Something had knocked the satellite internet out so I couldn't even get online.

I wanted to make a run for the intern's cabin, but going outside felt even more terrifying. Instead, I went back up to my room, sobbing, and huddled in the corner of my bed. I took two more Tylenol PMs and eventually fell asleep.

$$\triangle \ \triangle \ \triangle$$

I didn't wake up until almost 2:00 pm on Saturday. My head and stomach ached, and I felt awful. There were no signs that anyone had visited me the night before. Both porches looked fine; there weren't any muddy footprints or disturbances at the house. I tried the phones again but they didn't work. I then drove down to the interns' cabin but nobody was home. All the vehicles were gone.

I spent the rest of the day alternating between napping and reading. The storm had thrown the computers offline so I couldn't even get on the internet and email Mom or David. I didn't feel much like it anyway. I was just too exhausted.

Saturday night was uneventful. For the first time in weeks I didn't hear a single noise and slept as good as I could have.

On Sunday morning, however, I was awakened by another pounding on the door. *Oh my God, not again,* I moaned to myself. When I looked outside my window, however, I saw a police cruiser in the parking lot.

"What the hell?"

Throwing my robe on, I raced down the stairs and opened the front door. An officer was standing on the front porch, looking both stern and relieved at the same time. He was young, probably in his early thirties, and had the serious facial expression most officers have when they're confronting someone but aren't real sure as to how to proceed.

"Are you Miss Patrick?" he asked.

"Yes, that's me," I answered. I couldn't have broken the law. I hadn't been anywhere or done anything.

"I received a phone call from your mother this morning. She said the last she'd heard from you was Friday night. You were driving in a storm and got cut off. She hadn't heard from you the rest of the weekend. She was worried," he explained. He didn't say this accusingly, but it was obvious he was waiting for an explanation from me.

"Oh, man, I'm sorry," I apologized. "I called her from the gas station. I don't have a signal here and I can't call her from the phones here. The computer's down, too. I haven't felt well so I haven't been out all weekend."

"Well, it was right of her to worry. To be perfectly honest, I don't see why a young woman should be staying out here all by herself without access to communication," he said, furrowing his brows. "I wouldn't want my wife or daughter to do it."

I nodded. "Yeah, I'm not real thrilled about it either." I briefly filled him in on what happened the night before.

"Most likely someone playing a prank," he said. "Maybe the other staff members? But you need a phone here. Or a radio."

"Yeah, I know," I agreed.

I watched him drive away and then got dressed and drove into town.

New Arrivals

anet and the rest of the staff were not amused by the visit from the police which, of course, they heard about. Once I explained to them what had happened I felt a little foolish as well. At the time, it felt perfectly rational that my mother would call the only person she could think of to check on me and, given the circumstances, I could understand why she was worried. In the clear light of day with the farm house full of people and the phones and internet back online, however, it was difficult to remember just how isolating and unnerving the weekend had been. Only Janet was a parent herself; the rest of the women were either single or childless.

I also told them about the knocking and how I'd gone back and forth from one door to the other. While they'd all appeared disconcerted, each woman had a different explanation for what I'd probably heard. They all brushed it off. As it so happened, the interns had been off the grounds that night. They'd stayed in town with friends who had a house there. That news wasn't exactly settling.

"I have a job for you today," Tina approached me around noon.

I looked up from the computer where I'd been working on my budget. "What's up?"

"We have three staff members coming in by bus today and I need someone to go pick them up from the station. It's about an hour away and we've got a staff meeting. Would you like to go?" Since she was already handing me the keys to the company van it wasn't something I could exactly turn down. Besides, I loved the idea of getting out of the house.

"Sure!"

After printing off the directions I grabbed my purse and hit the road. I was picking up three international staff members: a guy from Scotland and two girls from the Czech Republic. All three were waiting for me when I reached the bus station.

"I'm sorry I'm late," I apologized when I got out of the van. "The traffic was heavier than I'd hoped."

"Not a very nice welcome or a good start to the summer," the Scottish guy grumbled as he loaded his bag into the back. The two girls rolled their eyes in unison and then stuck out their hands to me.

"I'm Merricka," the tall, thin blond with bright red lipstick and glittery earrings announced, "and this is Sarah. And we're starved. Can we get something to eat on the way? Please?"

The other girl was shorter, a brunette, and had a sunny smile. She wore a mini skirt and a Patsy Cline T-shirt. I liked both immediately.

"I'm hungry, too. Let's do it!" I said cheerfully. New possible friends. It wasn't going to be such a bad day after all.

The girls chattered about their plane ride, stay in Boston the night before, and bus to New Hampshire while the guy (John Paul) sulked and stared out the window with his arms crossed. Occasionally he'd sit up and take a picture and mumble something about a sight was "so American" before going back to his pose. The other two ignored him.

Our choices were limited to fast food so I pulled into a McDonalds since it was cheap and the one thing everyone knew. As we clamored out of the van Merricka clapped her hands and said, "I could eat three cheeseburgers I SWEAR!" Sarah nodded in agreement.

John Paul snorted. "No wonder everyone in America is so fat. With shit like this everywhere you just can't help it."

"How long have you been here?" I asked him, honestly curious.

"I got in yesterday," he shrugged.

I thought he was awfully jaded for someone who'd just arrived.

We ate inside and the girls chattered while John Paul nibbled on an order of fries. I was glad to have something different to eat myself. There weren't any fast food places anywhere near the resort so it was actually somewhat of a treat for me.

"When we get unpacked, can we come visit you tonight?" Sarah asked me as we got back in the van. "We need to start planning our summer. You've got a car and there are so many things we can do!"

"Like what?" I asked, because I was starting to feel some excitement. I liked the girls; they were fun.

"Um, like shopping!" Merikka sang. "And eating!"

"And beer!" Sarah laughed. "We love to drink!"

John Paul snorted. He was getting on my last nerves.

Before we got back on the road I stopped at a Wal-Mart and let the girls go in to buy some toiletries since it was their last chance. I went in with them to show them around but John Paul waited. "I wouldn't touch that sweat shop stuff," he scoffed. "Fucking American shit. No wonder everyone hates you."

"You've got a real attitude," I barked as I slammed the door. "Why did you come if you don't like anything?"

The girls had a good time in the store, though, and Sarah even bought herself a new bikini.

$$\triangle \ \triangle \ \triangle$$

Back at the grounds I introduced the new staff members to the office staff and the director got them settled into their quarters. Janet asked me how the drive had gone and I told her about John Paul's attitude and what I'd said to him. "I'm sorry, Janet, but he was rude and obnoxious and I just won't put up with that," I said.

"That's very strange," she mused. "He sounded so fun on the phone and had a great accent."

"I know," I agreed. "And I usually love Scotsmen."

I also told her about the Czech girls, though, and how they were going to hang out in my room that night. "Well, that's nice that you're meeting the kitchen staff but I hope you'll make friends with the other staff as well," she said strangely.

The comment left a bad taste in my mouth as I walked back to my desk and prepared to finish out the afternoon. What did it matter which part of the facility they worked in? I liked them.

$$\triangle \ \triangle \ \triangle$$

Evening rolled around and for the first time in weeks I wasn't feeling nervous about the setting sun. Just knowing there were more people around made me feel a little more secure. Even though there was obviously something going on in my own building, at least I was no longer completely alone. The thought made me feel braver and stronger. I sat down at my desk after making myself a sandwich for supper and wrote David a letter.

Dear David,

I made friends today. They're from Czech and I think we're going to get along just fine. The night sounds haven't started yet but I am not as nervous about them as I usually am. The new girls said they were going to come visit me tonight and I'm looking forward to it. I lugged the vacuum cleaner upstairs and cleaned my room a little. It's the most active I've been in weeks. For the first time in what feels like forever I'm starting to feel excited about being here. I haven't had girlfriends in a long time, at least not any my own age, and maybe this summer won't be as bad as I thought it was going to be. I don't want to put too much hope into this, but I really want our friendship to work out. It would be nice to have people to hang out with and I think we bonded.

Love,
Rebecca

Merricka and Sarah did come up as planned and the three of us sat on my bed, ate cookies, and listened to music for hours. I told them about my travels to Czech and showed them pictures of my mom and house back home. Sarah talked briefly of her pen pal, a guy from Alabama, and I told them about David and our letters and calls to one another. We giggled and laughed and for once there was nothing foreboding or sinister about the dark, shady attic room or shadowy mountaintop and surrounding forest. Instead, it almost felt cozy.

They'd been in the room for about two hours when the noises began.

"Who's that?" Sarah asked, curious, when the light footsteps approached the bedroom door.

I waited before answering, just to see what would happen. I didn't have to pause for long because seconds later the knob began turning and the door gently opened. Merricka gasped and jumped to her feet when nobody entered.

"What the–"Sarah thundered as she marched to the door and looked outside. "There's nobody here!"

"I know," I nodded. "It happens every night."

"We *all* heard that, right?" Sarah asked. "I'm not crazy going?"

"No," I agreed. "You're not crazy going. It sounds like someone walking."

The words were no sooner out of my mouth than a loud thump came from the room across the hall. Merricka shrieked and threw my pillow over her head and Sarah's face went pale. "For fuck!" she cried and slammed the door. "What *is* it?"

"I don't know," I answered honestly. "I think it's haunted."

"Yeah, a ghost, but who?" she asked. She was visibly trembling as she walked back over to the bed and sat down. "Did you see it?"

"No, I've never seen anything. Just the sounds. Well, a shadow once."

"Yeah, well," she began rummaging around in her purse for a cigarette and lit it. I refrained from pointing out the no smoking policy in the building. "I saw it. Not what but a shadow. Big and dark. Not good, my friend. This is not good."

The three of us sat there together without speaking, the silence only broken up by the muffled sounds outside. "It likes music," I finally volunteered. "A certain song."

I put the Nanci Griffith song on and the girls were duly impressed when the noises stopped. "I think it's a man. A young man. And he's sad. That's why the music soothes him. It's like a woman singing to him, like a lullaby," I tried to explain. "I don't know if it makes any sense, but I've spent a lot of time thinking about this."

"Do you know about bad things happening here? Happening in this house?" Merricka asked. She was on her second smoke.

"No. I asked Janet about the ghosts and she said nobody else had ever heard or seen anything. The interns said that's not true. I did ask her if anything bad had happened here and she said no."

"It's fucked up, it's shit," Sarah whispered. "How do you go to bed? I can't sleep. Maybe not tonight."

"Yeah, tell me about it," I muttered.

The mood became more subdued but at least I felt vindicated somewhat. I wasn't the only one hearing the sounds. I wasn't going crazy.

Vindication

espite the safety net I thought the Czech girls would bring, sleep was still hard to come by. The week hit me hard, even though Merricka, Sarah, and I got together every evening and talked. We did each other's makeup, listened to music, and talked about our future plans. And, we listened to the sounds.

"I'd go out of my *fucking* mind," Merricka seethed as she paced around my room. "Where is this sage? You need more."

I gave it to her and she used her lighter to set it ablaze. While Sarah and I went through my summer dresses Merricka waved it around the corners of the room and then through the stairwell, grumbling to herself in Czech. The thick white smoke filled the room and soon the three of us were coughing. I opened a window and tried to push some of it out while Sarah laughed. "Yes, put some outside! The whole fucking grounds need it. Get rid of the ghosts!"

Sleep evaded me for the next several days. The Tylenol had quit working. Warm chamomile tea and music did nothing to soothe me. I snapped at Kory again when she said something rude to me and even snapped at Janet when she told me I didn't have enough of a "smile" in my voice when I answered the phone. "I'm sorry," I'd snapped. "Is there a particular measurement of smile width you'd like for me to follow?"

Janet and Kory had looked at me, stunned, and then both had turned their backs on me and returned to their work. But I didn't get criticized about that again.

All I could think about was sleep. I tried to nap after work, but the girls would come and visit and not leave until nightfall. My idea of getting them to spend the night with me so that I didn't have to sleep in there alone didn't work. They'd have nothing to do with my bedroom.

"I'm torn, David," I moaned into the phone with him. "I'm scared as hell, but I'm also having fun with the girls. I've never been more terrified, or had so much fun, in my life I think. I've never had girlfriends before."

"Deep breaths, meditation. Try centering yourself," he advised. "I don't think what's there can hurt you, just get into your brain. Mind over matter and maybe you can deal with it."

Mind over matter, mind over matter, I repeated to myself when I was feeling particularly scared and thought I wanted to scream. People sought the supernatural, looked for them. Living with a ghost couldn't be so bad. I'd find new ways to sleep, new ways to ignore it. Or maybe I wouldn't ignore it at all. Maybe I'd learn to be friends with it. That might work, too, right? Like a "Ghost and Mrs. Muir" type thing?

Part of me hoped I could help the ghost/miserable spirit. It couldn't find the light or whatever. I'd guide it. Maybe I was there to give it peace. Maybe that's why I was there. But I didn't know how I could help it when I could barely help myself.

On Thursday I had to do inventory so, as a result, I got Friday afternoon off. Although I wanted to do nothing more than drag myself up the stairs and go to bed, I drove into town for lunch. I needed to get out of the farm house and make a store run anyway and it had been several days since I'd talked to my mother.

I wasn't feeling my best. I felt run down, fatigued. It was even hard taking a shower due to my lack of energy. I'd taken to wearing my hair in a ponytail and just slipping on jeans and T-shirts, when I'd usually wear dresses or skirts. I wasn't paying attention to how I looked. Most days I felt as though I was moving through the thick fog that often surrounded the farm house, like I was swimming through molasses. My effort was only put towards finding the energy to get through the day and, more importantly, the nights.

The night before I'd stepped outside my bedroom door to head downstairs to go to the bathroom and something across the hall had caught my eye in the empty room. It might have just been the way the light was reflecting from my own room, but for a second I was sure I saw the outline of a man standing in the middle of the floor, just looking at me.

I'd been so scared I could barely move and then it had simply faded away, just dissipated into thin air. If I'd had a container in my bedroom I might have turned right around and peed in it rather than face leaving the room.

At the tavern I must have looked as bad as I felt because when my favorite server approached me, she stopped dead in her tracks. "Oh, honey," she sang. "Are you sick? Are you okay?"

"That bad, huh?" I laughed weakly. I was so tired I wasn't even sure I could manage to eat, despite how empty my stomach had to have been. I'd barely eaten in two days.

"Well, you've looked rough before but this is about the worse. What's going on?" She looked so sincere, so caring, I couldn't help myself.

I was tired of pretending everything was okay and even though there were tables full of people around me and the room was a little on the quiet side, I spilled my guts to her. I started with the isolation and then told her about the sounds, my inability to sleep, and then ended with the fact that although things were certainly getting better as far as companionship went I still wasn't sure it was the job for me. I did not, however, tell her where I was working, what my job was, or even which town it was in.

During my speech she had stood there, hands on her hips, her eyes sympathetic and trusting. When I finished she sat down in the booth across from me and reached out and took my hands. With solemn eyes she said, "I believe everything you said about the ghosts. I think there's something in that place you're living in, I do. You look bad, honey, and it can't just be in your mind. I've seen and heard things, too. I know."

"Thank you," I whispered, grateful someone else believed me. Just getting it all off my chest again helped. I'd talked to the girls in my hostel, the woman in the Salem shop, and even the Czech girls at the resort but somehow talking to this woman was different. She'd seen me from the beginning. In a way, she'd been on this journey with me.

She smiled. "I just hope you're not living out on Bethlehem Road because that place is awful. I dated a guy out there once and it's got bad spirits. Awful ones. Not the good kind that you want around."

I looked at her with wide eyes. "That's *exactly* where I'm staying."

She turned a little pale. "You're not up at that farm house are you? The resort?"

"Yes," I nodded, eager. "*Yes!* Why?"

"Oh, God," she slapped her forehead. "Everyone around here knows about that place. That house is crazy haunted. All kinds of bad stuff. And that pond, too. Have you been to it? Honey, get out of there!"

"I went to the pond a few times," I said, a little unfocused. "I tried to walk around. Something didn't feel right."

"Of course it didn't," she agreed. "I've heard all kinds of stories about it. Things thrown in it, things buried at the bottom...even that it covers up some caves and burial grounds. But the farm house...that's another story."

"What happened there?" I asked excitedly. "Do you *know*? What is it?" Because I still felt if I could just figure out what "it" was, maybe I could learn to live with it... or make it go away.

"I don't know," she replied a little sadly. "But growing up, we used to even dare each other to walk up to it, go to the grounds when everything was closed. That's how bad of a reputation it has."

"Did you ever see anything there? Can you tell me?"

She nodded. "Once, when I was a teenager, I went up there with my boyfriend. It was March, maybe early April. Everything was closed. They don't have a caretaker living up there year-round, as you know. We poked around the pond but it was so dark and really foggy. I didn't like it. I made him leave. Then, as we were walking back to the parking lot I felt like someone was watching me. I kept turning around, looking behind me, but nobody was there. I started walking faster, just pulling him along. We got all the way to the car and I was about to get in when I heard this whisper. Just real soft-like. It called my name. My boyfriend at the time, he heard it too. We looked at each other and looked around us, but nobody was there. Then, I looked up. Up in one of those attic rooms, there was a person. The window was dark, but you could still see him. He was tall, thin, and looking down at us. He raised his hand and pressed it to the glass and looked right at me. Then he disappeared."

I shivered, envisioning exactly what she was talking about. "You got out of there, right?"

"Never went back again. Friends, though, they've heard crying, shouting, even singing. At the pond once a ball of light formed over the water and bounced around. Not light a lightening bug, but like fire. It's just *not* a good place."

I had no idea what to say. I was dumbfounded. Before I could get anymore words out, a middle-aged woman at the next table over spoke up. "Sweetie, I don't mean to eavesdrop, but I could hear what you were saying. And she's right. I've lived here all my life and I know that place. You shouldn't be staying there by yourself. And that house? Not good. If you're like this after a little over a month or two, heavens knows what will happen in four."

I suddenly found myself wanting to break down in tears. People believed me. I wasn't going crazy. The Czech girls had heard the sounds, these strangers were telling me to get out. It was like someone had opened the door for me and given me permission to be afraid and to walk away. I felt as though a weight had been lifted off my shoulders.

△ △ △

When I got back to the farmhouse the first person I encountered was Kory. She wasn't my first choice but she's who I had. "Kory," began without any niceties. "Did something happen in this house a long time ago? Something bad?"

Kory looked down at her feet, her long blond hair covering her face in sheets. At first, I didn't think she was going to respond. I continued to stand in front of her, though, my hands on my hips. "It's haunted, Kory, and not in a fun, Casper kind of way," I said. "I've been living here for more than a month and feel like I'm going out of my damn mind. Between the noises that won't let me sleep, the shadows, the lights, the sighs...It *never* stops. Janet said nobody else has ever heard or felt anything here, but I know that's not true. So be straight with me."

"Hey, you don't have to take that attitude with her," Tina admonished. She'd stolen into the room, as quiet as a mouse. Now she glared at me with steely eyes. I didn't care.

"I'm not trying to be rude," I said. "But somebody's going to talk. Do you want to do it?"

"I think we're all a little too old to be talking about ghosts," she scoffed.

"Okay, fine," I agreed. "Then it's not a ghost. But that makes it worse because it means someone has been playing pranks on me. Banging on the doors at night, climbing up and down my stairs, thumping around in the empty attic room after everyone's left...I don't see how that is any better." I was aware that my voice had gone up an octave. I was even feeling a surge of adrenalin. I needed to get myself under control.

"Okay, it is haunted," Kory said, jumping in before either Tina or I could say anything else. "And something *did* happen here."

"What?" I demanded.

"A long time ago. In the attic. A man, a teenager really, killed himself. He hung himself in that empty room," she said in a rush. "We used to put staff in that room, too, but nobody could sleep in there. That's why you're getting a roommate and they're not putting her in there by herself."

"Huh," I said, feeling a little vindicated. At one point it had felt like a man's presence. I was a little proud of myself for being right. "And I'm not the only one to hear things, feel things, see stuff?"

"No," Kory agreed. "You're not. Janet told me not to tell you about what happened there. About other people in the attic having problems."

"She told you not to tell me that, even after I asked her?"

"Yeah," Kory sighed. "I'm sorry." With that, she turned and walked out the door.

"It's not true," Tina declared. "Nobody killed themselves in that other room. Kory's just telling you that to make up a story, maybe make you feel like you're not crazy. Nobody else ever had a problem there." But she didn't say this very convincingly.

I stomped over to my desk and sat down to write two emails—one to my mother and one to David. I had a story now; at least the mystery was solved. Maybe *now* I could start dealing with what was going on.

△ △ △

The sun was setting behind the trees, the sky purple with streaks of red. I could see the pond from my window and shivered at the implications my server had made. What was in there? Was it just an urban legend? My bedroom door was open, inviting. I expected the Czech girls to come visiting soon. The room across the hall was already deep in shadows. A thin pale light ran from my room, down the short hallway, and flooded the doorway. Like a trail of breadcrumbs, it seemed to welcome whatever was in there, possibly lead it right to my door. I didn't care that night.

I'd already burned some sage and cleansed my room again. A line of salt was laid across my doorframe; nobody could supposedly enter if they meant me harm. I'd meditated over a necklace I bought in Boston and wore it as a talisman to offer more protection. Now I stood by my door, my hand on my knob, and watched the dark room across from me.

"Hello?" I called, doing my best to keep my voice steady. "Are you there?"

Nothing happened.

"I know what happened to you," I said. "And I'm sorry. You must have felt sad, empty. Maybe you didn't know what to do. I've felt that way, too. I'm sorry you felt this was the best option for you. And I know this is your home and I'm an intruder here, but you can't keep scaring me. I don't know that I can help you. You know the way you felt before you died? I'm starting to feel that way, too. And I don't want to. You have to give me a break, cut me some slack."

The house remained quiet, but the pale light that once reached to the other door now started dissolving. As I watched in dismay, a dark shadow edged over it, creeping inch by inch until most of the line was gone. I could feel eyes on me, someone or something looking not only at me but through me, inside of me.

Was there something standing across from me, mere feet away, studying me from their doorway as I tried to study it?

The hair on the back of my neck stood up at point and cold chills ran down my arms. My instinct was to slam my door and lock myself inside, but I couldn't make myself move.

"It's not just the noises, I might be able to live with that, but you're *always* here, always watching me and messing with me. It makes me nervous. I'm scared. I don't know how to help you. I don't know what to do. So I want you to just leave me alone."

The last word was no sooner out of my mouth then the door to the empty room slammed shut with a force that made my own door quiver in its frame. The pale line of light reappeared now, unhampered by whatever had made it vanish.

Moments later, two sets of footsteps came running up the stairs. I could hear Merricka and Sarah panting. "Are you okay?" Merricka called as the neared the top. They were staying in a cabin on the other side of the resort and had already walked nearly half a mile to reach me at the farm house.

"We heard a loud bang," Sarah wheezed.

"It's just my neighbor," I pointed to the closed door. "I don't think he wanted to play."

The girls talked me into going out that night, drinking with them at a local bar. I obliged, but I didn't drink. When I returned home the door to the empty room was open again. Nothing changed. The whispers and thuds against my door, if anything, grew louder.

It doesn't care that it's bothering me, I told myself as I pulled my blanket up over my face. *I think it likes the fact that it's driving me insane.*

Changes

I thought *knowing* would help me deal with what was going on.

It didn't.

That first night, I turned my music up and was actually able to ignore the sounds. I did okay on the second night, too. When I came out of the shower after work and heard a loud "thump" above me, I ignored it. Singing to myself, I nonchalantly walked up the stairs, paying no mind to the light footsteps that paced back and forth across the hall. I let myself into my room, smiled, and closed the door. Then I collapsed on the bed. But it was progress. I had a good four hour stretch of sleep without waking up and didn't even flinch when I went to the bathroom in the middle of night, in spite of loud exhale that filled the stairwell when I started down it.

A sad man, I told myself. *A man who couldn't deal with whatever was in his heart and found a long-term solution to a short-term problem.*

Above, a crash and moan amplified my thoughts. It was quiet after that.

But the next day, after work, I had another kind of surprise. As I let myself up the stairs and started towards my door, a nasty surprise met me. I nearly stepped on it but just happened to look down at the last moment and caught myself. The whole house could've heard my scream, had anyone else been in it.

There, neatly placed where I couldn't possibly miss it, was a mutilated rat. It wasn't just dead; it had been cut into at least four parts. The blood pooled and ran under my door in thick lines.

I vomited twice as I cleaned it up. And I swore I could hear the faint tinkling of laughter.

The next evening, after taking the Czech girls to the movies, I returned to find a dead bird in the same position. It was so mutilated, I couldn't even tell what kind of bird it had been.

"Maybe someone plays bad joke?" Sarah demanded in disgust. They helped me clean this one up.

"Maybe," I replied. "But that's pretty sick."

I informed Janet of the dead bird and rat. "Maybe they ate some poison," she shrugged. "We DO lay out traps around here."

"And cut itself into several pieces afterwards?" I countered.

She didn't have an answer for that.

John Paul, the Scotsman, came in later that afternoon. "I'm in some serious need of cash," he demanded as he marched up to my desk.

"You and me both, buddy," I laughed.

"I'm not your 'buddy,'" he retorted.

"Geeze, relax," I sighed. "It's just an expression. What do you need?"

"Cash, I told you. Are you deaf?"

Highly offended, I sat back and glared at him. "Um, first of all, you don't need to speak to me in that tone. And secondly, as much as I'd like to have a wad of hundreds stuck behind my ear, I don't. What exactly do you want me to do about your situation?"

"Don't you have some petty cash in your desk you could give me?" he gestured towards my drawers.

"No, they don't give me that kind of money. Do you need something for the resort?"

"No, I need to go out tonight," he whined.

"Well, you definitely couldn't use petty cash for that," I advised. "But go talk to Tina. She might be able to give you an advance on your paycheck or something."

He stomped out, muttering under his breath. I heard the word "bitch." Maybe Sarah was right. Maybe someone was playing a bad joke on me. He was a good candidate.

An hour later, Kory sauntered into the office and approached me. "Janet told me I need to train you on how to use the fax machine."

"Oh, it's okay, she showed me on my first day," I said. "I've got it."

"Yes, but there are certain procedures you need to know. Like how to address a fax, how to fill out a form, what kind of heading to use."

"Isn't there a fax cover sheet? I thought I saw a stack of them here," I said, confused.

"Yes, but you have to make sure your spelling is good, that you use proper grammar. I'm meant to train you on that."

I must have looked at her like she had two heads because she took a step back. "So you're not going to train me on how to send a fax...you're here to train me on how to spell correctly?"

She nodded.

"Kory, let me ask you all a question...Why did you hire me? I thought it was because I had eight years of office experience. I started working as the assistant to an executive director when I was seventeen years old. I can understand being trained when it comes to where things are, how to use programs that are exclusive to your organization, and what your protocols are. But these are not things I'm being trained on. Instead, I'm being trained on how to talk on the phone, how to use a stapler, and how to dust. Did anyone actually read my resume when I was hired?"

Her mouth dropped open a few inches and then her lips curled in anger. "You don't have to be so rude to me," she snapped.

"I knew that when I was hired here it was to do some general office work, but I'm barely doing that. In fact, I get treated like I'm an idiot," I snapped back.

"Well, some of it is the way you speak."

"You mean my attitude?"

"No, the way you pronounce your words," she chided. "Janet and Linda are afraid to have you on the phone. Customers can't understand you. We were going to work with you on that."

I was stunned. "I'm from the south," I muttered. "I'm not losing my accent just because someone from the north doesn't understand me. Nobody's ever had trouble before."

I excused myself then and stalked outside. Merricka was sitting on the porch, waiting for Sarah. One look at my face showed her I was upset. "Are you okay?" I told her what had transpired.

"Oh God!" she seethed. "You're one of the only people here I can understand at all! They are just being mean. Just mean."

"I don't know what's worse," I mumbled. "The ghosts or the people."

△ △ △

That night I was getting ready to bed when a low grumbling sound filled the room. It started low, like the beginning of a clap of thunder, and steadily grew louder until my walls began to shake. An earthquake?

I ran to my window and looked outside, but nothing was moving. It was just inside. Behind me, my doorknob began rattling, the door shaking in its frame as though trying to open on its own. I ran to it and placed my hands on the wood. It was burning hot, like it had been outside in the sun all day. Then another horrific thought struck me. A fire? Oh God! But the knob was cool to the touch. It was just the wood that was hot.

"Stop it!" I called, banging on the door. "Stop it!"

The door vibrated in response, the heat now coming off it in waves. I could actually see them.

Probably not my best move, but not knowing what else to do, I gave the door a tug and flung it open. The door across the hall was closed but when I took a step outside it started inching over, faster and faster. I couldn't stay and watch so I turned and began clamoring towards the stair. Two steps down, though, and the overhead light blew above me, sending the stairwell into almost total darkness. The door at the bottom was shut, something I didn't remember doing, and I picked up speed, feeling for the banister for balance. Above me, I could hear footsteps picking up their pace; it was following me.

A few steps from the bottom I reached for the doorknob I knew was there when what felt like a ton of pressure pushed me from behind. Losing my balance, I tumbled towards the door, banging my head on the wood with a clunk. My hand found the knob, though, and I fell off the stairs, face first, onto the landing.

Dazed, I lay there on the floor, my face pressed against the cool tiles. The footsteps had stopped. The room beyond kept fading from light to dark. My head was pounding. *Well*, I thought, *maybe I'll just lay here for a minute and take a little nap.*

Sarah and Merricka found me. They helped me up and led me back up the stairs where the two of them mothered me and put me to bed. I had a large bump on my head and my leg was bleeding. I'd cut it on the wooden stairs somehow. They cleaned this, too.

"You get out tomorrow," Merricka chided. "You tell them to let you move to another place."

I nodded my head in agreement. "I need to go email David," I said woozily.

"You do it later," Sarah said. "He will understand. We will stay for a long time with you."

When I woke up at midnight and, again at 3:00 am, they were still there. They were still there the next morning, too, when it was time to go to work. They were huddled together on my floor, my bathrobe wrapped around them.

$$\triangle \ \triangle \ \triangle$$

"What's on your head?" Janet asked. She didn't sound particularly interested, though.

"I fell down the stairs last night," I said. "Or something pushed me."

"I don't think we've ever had someone so clumsy," she mused. "Isn't this the second time you've done that?"

"The light blew out. It was dark."

"Hmmm..."

I went about my filing and later dropped a note to David and Mom. David was looking at airline tickets again. He was ready to book his. I couldn't wait to see him. I wanted him there now. I'd glossed over the incident from the night before in my email to him, but I planned on going out later and calling him to tell him all about it. Merricka and Sarah were enthralled with our relationship; they wanted pictures, they wanted details, and they wanted to meet him. "He's a little like a dream," Sarah had cooed after glancing at one of his messages to me. "He's so caring."

"It is my dream to meet an American man," Merricka admitted. "Maybe one from the south with a mansion."

"You and me both, girlfriend," I laughed.

I couldn't believe how much better I was feeling, despite the horror from the night before. Just having friends and girls I could talk and laugh with was enough to lift my spirits. I briefly wondered if that's why the attic was mad. Maybe because it wasn't pulling me in as hard as it had been. Misery loves company, after all.

I'd taken time with my looks that morning. I was tired of looking and feeling tired all the time. I applied my makeup with care, picked out a matching skirt and top and low heels, and even curled my hair. I felt and looked a little more like my "old" self, even the self before all the sadness back in Kentucky.

Despite my pounding head and the scratch on my leg that really hurt more than it should have, the morning flew by. The filing and emails gave me something to do. I was looking at hostels in Vermont, too, for the weekend. It was time to branch out and try a state I'd never visited. Why not take that opportunity while I was here?

I can do this, I cheered myself on, *I can still make this a fabulous summer*. Ghost be damned.

After lunch, Janet and Linda, the director, called me into Linda's office. I gathered up my courage. Now was the time to demand I be moved. I wasn't staying another night in that attic. Enough was enough. If nothing else, the injury should've worked in my favor.

When I walked in, Linda pointed to a spot on her couch. I sat there while Janet sat beside me. Linda sat across from us in a rolling chair. Both doors to her office were wide open and other staff members walked by, their chattering filling the air. Both women had pleasant looks on their faces, but neither one had smiles that reached their eyes.

"Rebecca," Linda began with what sounded like false cheer, "we need to talk to you."

"Okay," I declared brightly, folding my hands in my lap and trying hard not to twist them. Perspiration was gathering under my arms and running down my sides in streaks. I could never stay dry when I was nervous. Fabrics that didn't breathe were not my friends. "There's some things I need to talk about, too."

Linda looked down at her Birkenstocks and bit her lip.

"We've discussed everything and we just feel this is not the right place for you," Janet pronounced in a hurry. I could detect the faintest of smiles whispering across her pursed lips.

What?

"We've talked to the other staff and, the fact is, you're just not getting along with anyone. People think you're rude, and not nice, and we just can't have that kind of attitude here," Linda continued for Janet. She tried to look regretful, but it wasn't working. "This is supposed to be a fun place with a relaxed atmosphere. You're just not fitting in."

What?

I didn't even know where to begin with that. "Not everyone feels that way," I pointed out at last. "I've made friends with some of the kitchen staff."

The two women exchanged looks and Linda even raised her eyebrows slightly, a move that infuriated me. I resented the implication that, because they were foreign and worked in the kitchen, they somehow didn't count. True, they weren't pot smoking interns, but I liked them.

"Well," Janet disclosed, leaning forward, "we've talked to them, too, and explained that you have some health concerns that affect your attitude and we just can't keep you on anymore."

My eyes just about boggled right out of my head. "What?" I laughed. "Are you serious? What 'health concerns?' And even if I did, wouldn't that violate some kind of HIPPA policy? To discuss health problems with people I didn't give you permission to?"

They stared at me like I was speaking another language. Kory walked by the office then and peeked in at us. Janet smiled at her before she hurried on.

"This makes no sense to me," I muttered.

"And another thing," Janet added. "You always look too happy to leave on Fridays. You're always going out of town. Like you don't want to be here."

"Hey," I squealed. "You told me in my interview that being able to travel in the surrounding area and sightsee was a perk of this location. And, I'm sorry, but it's Friday! Everyone is happy to have a few days off."

"We're very sorry, but we'll need you to leave today," Linda said with resolution.

"It's 3:00 pm," I sputtered. "I live five states away. We don't get paid for another week. You haven't provided my meals or given me a place to cook so I've had to eat out almost every day. There hasn't been a chance to save much money, especially not enough to drive all the way back right now and stop along the way, which is what I'll have to do since I'm alone. Where the hell am I supposed to go?"

The women looked at one another as though this thought hadn't crossed their minds.

"I'm sorry, but you'll just have to leave," Janet sighed. "You're belligerent and mean-spirited. We've tried being kind to you but you won't have any of it."

She didn't mention the ghosts, my falling, or any of the issues I'd brought up to her. The fact of the matter was, I was too much work for them. Much like the ghost had disrupted my life, I was disrupting theirs. The ghost had been my parasite, eating off me and sponging my energy. In some way, I had done the same to them. Maybe it was my fault, maybe it wasn't. In the end, it didn't matter.

There was no use arguing. They were giving me an out. I would have to go home now. I would have to face the fact that I'd tried this job, tried to do something different for myself, and had failed. I wasn't as upset as I thought I'd be. Oh, I was mad as hell, but at least I could leave. That decision, having been taken out of my hands, was no longer mine. It was freeing, in a way.

Having nothing left to say, and no energy left to waste on people who obviously didn't want me, I got up and paraded out of the room and stalked to my desk, my head held high as other staff members pretended not to watch. As I began putting my personal belongings in a box, I picked up the office phone and called my mother. I didn't care that it was on their dime.

"Mom?" I began as soon as she answered. "I'm coming home. I got fired."

"What?" she cried. "Why!?"

"Probably because the light went out in the stairs and I fell down it, again, and they just don't want to deal with me anymore. And they say I'm mean and nobody likes me."

"Keep your voice down," Janet hissed from behind me.

"Oh, stop," I snapped back, not even looking at her. "I'm not making a scene. You're the one who fired me with the office door open and everyone walking by, trying not to listen. And telling my friends I had 'health concerns?' Lady, you're lucky I'm not calling a lawyer right now."

I went back to the conversation with my mother. "Look, I'm sorry but I need help with money. They did this to me a week before pay day. I have the gas to get home, but little else. Can you make me a hotel reservation for Hartford for tonight? I'll stop there on the way."

"Yes, but I'd be pissed," she seethed. "What do they think they're doing?"

"It's okay, Mom," I said wearily. "This isn't the place for me. I'm not this person. I just need to come back."

"Just be careful," she advised. "The only important thing is that you're coming home." Her voice sounded lighter, relieved.

With that, I grabbed my belongings from my desk, turned around, and trooped out of the office and up the stairs. I wouldn't have to look at any of them again.

△ △ △

Merricka and Sarah cried while I stuffed clothing into my suitcases. "I can't believe you're going," Sarah wailed. "It's mean. No fair. You're the only person we *like*."

"It's for the best," I sighed. They were trying to help me pack, but both sat on my bed, heads low, looking dejected. "I'm sorry I won't be here to take us to the beach and movies."

"We had plans for the summer," Merricka moaned. "We were going to have fun."

"I know," I said sadly. I could feel a few glimmers of tears filling my eyes. They threatened to spill over, so I tried to rub them away. "I was starting to look forward to it, too. But you know I can't stay here. Look at what's happening. I'm going out of my mind. That thing, that boy, he won't leave me alone. He's eating at me. By the end of the summer, I might not even recognize myself. I came here in bad shape, but the place, it's making me worse. They wouldn't move me. Getting rid of me is best. They just don't want to deal with me anymore."

"It's not fair," Sarah said again.

The door across the hall slammed, as if in agreement.

Leaving

We went to dinner one last time, "my" pub. I said goodbye to my little waitress again. "I'm glad you're going," she said. "It was no place for you, for anyone really."

Afterwards, while the other two girls smoked out on the dock, I called up David.

"I feel like a failure for coming home," I said.

"You're not going home," he chuckled. "You're coming to see me."

"Yeah, well..."

"This is different from your other job. You stuck with it, you tried," he pointed out. "Hell, you tried with the other one."

"I know," I sighed. "I feel like I let everyone down, though."

"It wasn't your fault that you were sexually harassed," he said.

Every time he said the words, or I thought them, a sick feeling ran through me. "Sexually harassed." What a weird phrase. A phrase that could mean so many things. Had I been harassed? What if I'd just been overreacting? What if he hadn't meant anything about the way he'd leered at me, told me that he wanted a good fuck? That the people in town were so religious that they probably wouldn't even notice anything was going on? About the way he'd touch my thigh, brush against my breast?

Hadn't it all been harmless? I wasn't physically hurt. He didn't rape me. In a fight, I probably could have taken him; he was a soft, pudgy man who was slow on his feet and didn't seem to have quick reflexes. He hadn't threatened to fire me if I didn't sleep with him, hadn't cornered me in some dark room once everyone else left.

And yet...I'd still felt painfully violated. Not just sexually, but emotionally. I'd liked him, had fully trusted in the idea that he was just a great guy who cared about his employees. I'd been proud that someone so kind and caring had been my boss.

And he'd violated that.

And boy, did I ever regret telling my immediate supervisor about what had happened. I still wish I'd kept my mouth shut. What he had done was bad; what everyone else did that followed was worse. When the other two young women came forward and said that they'd been harassed as well, all hell had broken loose. The other girls in our organization avoiding us, later telling us that they'd been instructed not to eat lunch with us or hang out with us. The bullying by the other women. The constant write ups. I'd gone from being a star employee to getting in trouble for not only tiny things that I did wrong but for many things that I hadn't done at all.

The things they'd said to me had become so bad that I'd started wearing a tape recorder around my neck.

"It's a good thing this happened to you, Rebecca, and not some other girl," I was told. "What if it had been someone with a husband or boyfriend? Think of what would've happened if we'd had an irate spouse down here?"

Yeah, I was so "lucky."

"I would've come up there," David had said when I'd told him that. "I still will if you want me to."

Still, I'd hung in there. Afraid to leave. Afraid of letting go because I didn't know what the future held. I'd hung in there until I was basically paid off to go away and keep my mouth shut. Now, six months later, I was learning that the business was closing altogether, that my boss had been investigated for missing money or something.

This time, at least, the choice was made for me.

△ △ △

The air was dense and full as I pulled away from the farm house. There was no sunset, the sky was just bleached. A light mist covered my windshield, chilled me. I turned the heat on "low" and let the warmth cover me and fill me, inside and out. The trees were motionless. They were just starting to fill out with green leaves, but in the fog they looked brown, murky. The air wasn't so much still as it was stagnant. A smell I'd never noticed before rose from the ground, fell from the sky, and tried to wrap around me and the car. It was old and unpleasant. My stomach was turning a little and I felt like I could vomit.

The farm house rose up behind me, a sentinel. I knew Merricka and Sarah were on the front porch, sitting in the rocking chairs, waving at me. They'd helped me carry everything down. Sarah wore a bright pink top and Merricka had on light blue shorts. When I'd last looked at them on the porch they'd been beacons of light, their vibrancy fighting the murkiness and shadows. But the fog was starting to close in on them, too.

My mother was waiting for me. I wouldn't get there until late the next night, but no matter the time she'd be sitting up in the living room, the light on for me with something ready to eat. And David was waiting. I just had to give the word and he'd be there. I was ready to quit for a while, to let someone else fuss over me and make some trouble over me. I was tired but strengthened.

I tried not to look back; tried only to push forward on the gas and forget about what had happened there. But I couldn't help it.

Adjusting my mirror, I slowed down and gazed backwards. The girls were still on the porch, still waving. I looked up. I could see the window of my attic room clearly. It watched me pull away. And as I watched *it*, the lamp flickered on and the room filled with light.

Afterword

The drive back home was long; it felt even longer than the thirteen hours it took me. I only vaguely remember parts of it. I pulled over into a youth hostel in Hartford, Connecticut and spent the night in an old, ramshackle house and then got up early the next morning and drove the rest of the way straight through. Somewhere in Pennsylvania I slept in the front seat of the car at a rest area until the sun got too hot beating in through the windows.

I didn't feel as defeated as I thought I would. I'd tried my best, but just wasn't strong enough to work or live in that environment. It wasn't the place for me, even without the ghost.

Upon returning home I took a few weeks to readjust and pack my bags for Wales and then I got on a Greyhound bus and took off for Florida. It took me almost thirty-six hours to travel down the coast, but David was waiting for me there. I spend the rest of the summer recovering, relaxing, and recuperating. He provided me with a sanctuary and the friendship I needed.

We spoke little of what transpired in the farm house. He'd already heard most of it by the time I arrived. Over the course of the next few months I tried to forget it. I wanted to move forward. In fact, in time the events even began fading from my mind. Had it not been for the letters I sent home and the diary I kept I might have been able to forget the details and pretend it never happened, that it had all been a nightmare.

I left for Wales in October.

To get to my university town I had to fly into London, take a three-hour train ride to Cardiff, transfer to a small town called Carmarthen, take a one-hour bus ride to MY town, and ride a pack mule the rest of the way. (Just kidding about the mule part...sort of.)

Of course, the airline lost my luggage. I had nothing but my laptop and a small carry-on which, thanks to FSA guidelines, allowed me very little. Naturally, it was raining and frigid and I'd packed my coat in my suitcase so that I didn't have to keep up with it on the plane.

By the time I arrived at the university I'd been traveling for almost twenty-four hours. It was dark; I was cold and wet. When I found my way to the front office, I was informed that since it was so late they'd "accidentally" given my room away. Swell.

"No worries, love," the cheerful porter sang. "I'll find you a room!" He loaded me up on a golf cart and drove me to a nearby dorm. There, he began opening doors at random, trying to find me one that hadn't been taken.

While he was doing this, I became aware of a tall, very good-looking guy standing in the hallway. He was movie-star handsome with bright blue eyes and blond, curly hair. I was worn out and looked like a drown rat. My laptop was heavy. "Excuse me," the porter said to him. "Can she put her bags in your room until we find her one?"

The guy's name was Pete and he was waiting for his friends. They were getting ready to go out to dinner to celebrate their first semester of graduate school. The porter found me a room five doors down from him.

Several weeks went by and we quickly developed a friendship. We shared a kitchen and I found that I was hanging out in it more and more, hoping to see him. Of course, whenever I went in there I was always in full makeup, cute clothes, and had great-looking hair. It wasn't suspicious at all at 2am!

I kept up this charade for almost a month. And then I got a job picking carrots at an organic farm. Since I hadn't finished my contract at the resort, I'd arrived in Wales with very little money and it became essential that I pick up some work. I'd applied for several positions but, so far, only the farm had replied with an offer.

It was dirty, uncomfortable work. The muck and grime would cling to my skin and hair and the thick gloves and Wellingtons I wore did little to protect my hands and feet from the mud and cold. I came home every day and quickly jumped into the shower before anyone could see me. The farm was beautiful, but carrot picking is no joke; it's a lot of work!

One day, though, the weather was particularly miserable. It was raining, cold, and the mud was so thick it came up to my knees. I could barely see for the torrential rain and my hands were freezing before I'd even stuck them in the ground.

When we got to the field, I hopped off the tractor and started to take a step forward and...SPLAT! *I* moved but my feet did not. I wound up face down in the mud. I was mortified. The owners carted me home where I HOPED I could sneak in and clean up before anyone saw me.

It was then I realized I'd locked myself out of my dorm room.

A call to housekeeping told me they could be there in half an hour. Nobody else was around so I tried to hide in the corner of the kitchen, keeping quiet.

Pete wandered in ten minutes later.

To his credit, he didn't laugh in my dirt-streaked face but he DID offer to let me use his shower and put on one of his T-shirts until housekeeping arrived.

It was when he saw me, mud and all, that he says he realized he was in love with me. I'd known a little sooner.

Two years later, we gave birth to our first child. We married, moved back to the United States together upon graduation, and (for the most part) lived happily ever after.

About the Author

Rebecca Patrick-Howard is the author of several books including the paranormal mystery series *Taryn's Camera*. She lives in eastern Kentucky with her husband and two children. To order copies of ALL of Rebecca's books, including autographed paperbacks, visit her website at:

www.rebeccaphoward.net

Let's Connect!

Pinterest: https://www.pinterest.com/rebeccapatrickh/
Website: www.rebeccaphoward.net
Email: rphwrites@gmail.com

Facebook: https://www.facebook.com/rebeccaphowardwrites
Twitter: https://twitter.com/RPHWrites
Instagram: https://instagram.com/rphwrites/

Book Excerpt:

Two Weeks: A Family's True Haunting

TWO WEEKS

A True Haunting

Rebecca Patrick-Howard

S

he needed to get out of the tub, she needed to grab her towel, but that would mean turning her head and looking at the door. The thought of what might be there stunned her in fear, the most vivid sensation she'd ever felt. "Daddy," she whimpered, praying he'd be able to hear her thoughts and come to her. She thought of calling out downstairs, bringing up one of her siblings, but her throat was tight. She didn't think she could holler if she tried.

With slow, easy movements she lifted herself from the tub and grabbed the towel on the back of the toilet. The softness felt good on her skin, its weight a shield against whatever was out there. Feeling stronger now she slowly turned to face the door, her eyes clenched shut and her teeth grinding against each other.

With determined resolution she gathered all the courage she'd ever had, thinking about the super heroes in movies she loved, and opened her eyes to what was waiting for her.

The figure that stood before her was just a few feet away. If they'd both stretched out their hands they could've touched one another. The long hair, dark dress that brushed the floor and delicate hands could only belong to a woman. Where her face should've been, however, there was nothing but a pale void.

"Ahhhhkkkkk!!!!" Laura screamed, her voice returning in a ferocious roar. "Dad-EE!"

The figure gave out a solitary hiss, like a balloon running out of air, and disappeared.

Laura was still standing wet in the middle of the bathroom floor when Jimmy and Jenny found her. Shaking and crying, they led her to her bedroom where Jenny petted on her and helped her dress. Jimmy marched up and down the hallway, checking closets, looking under beds, and making sure all the windows were locked.

There was no question about whether they believed Laura. They both knew now, for sure, that their new house was haunted.

Available Now!

Other Books by Rebecca

To see ALL of Rebecca's books and to order both eBooks AND signed paperback versions, visit her website at:

www.rebeccaphoward.net

Taryn's Camera Series

Windwood Farm (Book 1)
The locals call it the "devil's house" and Taryn's about to find out why!

Griffith Tavern (Book 2)
The old tavern has a dark secret and Taryn's camera's going to learn it soon.

Dark Hollow Road (Book 3)
Beautiful Cheyenne Willoughby has disappeared. Someone knows the truth.

Shaker Town (Book 4)
Taryn's camera is finally revealing a past to her that she's always longed to see-the mysterious Shakers as they were 100 years ago. But is she seeing a past she hadn't bargained for?

Jekyll Island (Book 5)
Jekyll Island is known for its ghosts, as well as its fascinating history, but now the two are about to take Taryn on a wild ride she'll never forget!

Black Raven Inn (Book 6)
The 1960's music scene…vibrant, electrifying, and sometimes even deadly…

Muddy Creek (Book 7)
Lucy did a bad, bad thing when she burned down the old school. Now it's up to Taryn to find out why.

Bloody Moor (Book 8)
The call it "the cursed" and the townspeople still fear the witch that reigned there a century ago. But this haunted Welsh mansion has more than meets the eye!

Sarah's House (Book 9)

When Taryn inherited the old, rambling house from her beloved aunt Sarah, she never knew that she'd find herself in the middle of a mystery-and friends with a ghost!

Taryn's Pictures: Photos from Taryn's Camera
Taryn's Haunting

A Broom with a View
She's your average witch next door, he's a Christmas tree farmer with sisters named after horses. Kudzu Valley will never be the same when Liza Jane comes to town!

Broommates
When Bryar Rose makes a fool of herself on national television, it's time for her to return to Kudzu Valley. But now that she's accused of murdering half the town, will anyone truly accept her?

A Broom of One's Own
What does a witch do when she can't get rid of the restless spirit that haunts the old cinema? Call for backup! (A Taryn's Camera/Kentucky Witches crossover)

Nothin' Says Lovin' Like Something from the Coven

Furnace Mountain: Or the Day President Roosevelt Came to Town
When Sam Walters invited the president to visit his Depression-era town, he never dreamed of what would happen next!

The Locusts (Coming Soon)

Things She Sees in The Dark
Mallory's cousin was kidnapped when she was eight years old and Mallory saw the whole thing happen. She's suffered amnesia ever since. Now, 25 years later, her memories are starting to return. Can she solve the case that no detective has been able to crack? And will she live through it, if she does?

Haunted Estill County
More Tales from Haunted Estill County
Haunted Estill County: The Children's Edition
Haunted Madison County
A Summer of Fear
The Maple House
Four Months of Terror
Two Weeks: A True Haunting
Three True Tales of Terror
The Visitors

Other Books

Coping with Grief: The Anti-Guide to Infant Loss
Three Minus Zero
Finding Henry: One Woman's Solo Quest to Find Love, Life, & Crepes in Eastern Europe
Estill County in Photos
Haunted: Ghost Children Stories from Beyond
Haunted: Houses

WINDWOOD FARM excerpt

Book 1 in Taryn's Camera

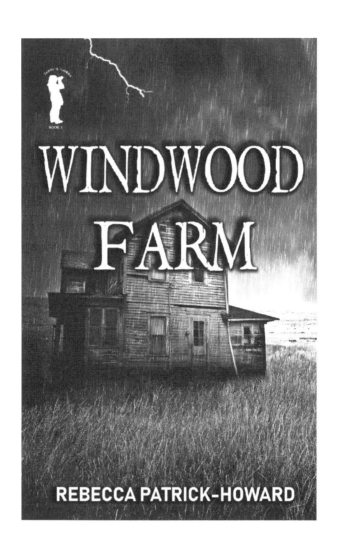

She might depend on her eyes for most of her work, but it was her strong sense of smell that often accosted her first; the scent of death never fully left a place. As Taryn slowly drove down the long, loosely graveled driveway, taking careful observation of her surroundings, she was immediately hit by the overpowering aroma of devastation. It was an old scent and one covered up by others along the way but the closer she got to the house, the more quickly the layers peeled back until she was almost crying inside her old Dodge.

Fighting the urge to either burst into tears or throw up, she struggled to close off that part of her mind and ignore the stench and instead tried to focus on what was ahead. First impressions were always the most important to her in this job because that's when she saw the big picture. She would never fully get it again. Later, once she had grown accustomed to the place and her surroundings, she would pay careful attention to the details and the little nuances she often fell in love with. But it was the first look that usually hit her the hardest.

Taryn was not disappointed in the view. The low green hills and golden valleys spread out before her in all directions, giving her a panorama of beautiful countryside in the morning sun. She wasn't much of a morning person, but she did have an appreciation for the light offered early in the day; the land was cast with a faint yellow glow then, as though the fields had been set on fire. It wouldn't happen again until sunset. The long driveway rambled off the main road and dipped down over a small rise and at the bottom of the hill there were woods she imagined led to the next farm. The trees were thick, dark and mysterious, adding to the ambience. She was glad that at least not everything was being developed around here, but how long would that last? Off in the distance, she saw the low rising buildings of town, creeping deliberately toward the farm in their urban sprawl, getting closer and closer as if they were ready to spring at any moment and capture the last remaining remnants of the farmland that lingered. Soon, it would be difficult to see any fields at all.

That was partly why she was there.

The grounds were well-kept with their sweet-smelling grass thick and low and wild roses growing up wooden plank fences faded almost white in the summer sun.

With her windows down, she could smell hay and the air was hot; sticky-sweet already and it was barely June. Someone was taking care of the property and not letting it get overgrown. That was good. Hopefully it meant there wouldn't be too many snakes. She didn't do snakes.

The barns and smaller outbuildings caught her eye before the house. They were in disrepair but stood solidly despite missing several key structural frames. A chicken coop had seen better days and was lopsided, but it was trying. She applauded its tenacity. The barn looked downright sturdy. She recalled seeing a leaning barn outside of Cleveland that rivaled the tower in Pisa, and this barn didn't look as if it were going anywhere anytime soon, either. It was weathered and bleached in the sun, and several boards were missing, but she could easily imagine it filled with equipment and horses, their hooves beating on the dirt floor, ready to get the morning started. She loved exploring barns, even the unsafe ones. Perhaps because she'd grown up in the city, she'd always felt a calling for the countryside and enjoyed herself whenever she was in it.

The house itself was set before her, peeking stoically out from behind two overgrown oak trees, their branches reaching up into the sky as if in prayer and their leaves full, almost overpowering the house.

It was a timeworn stone structure, built in 1849, with an addition thoughtlessly tacked on the back. That part was painted a dingy white, the paint flaked off through the years, leaving it pock-marked and naked. Nobody ever bothered to fix it, that she could tell. Indeed, the house hadn't been lived in since the 1930s for reasons that hadn't yet been explained to her.

Dense, feminine, ivy with delicate fingers curved her nails around the front doors but it didn't really matter since the doors were nailed shut with thick, ugly wooden planks that peeked grotesquely through the vines.

The fact that the house was constructed of stone was part of what set it apart from other houses built during the same era; the fact that the architect had gone on to achieve some critical acclaim was another. A young man when he designed this house, he went on to design several more in Washington, D.C. and New York City and then won the A1A Gold Medal, awarded by the American Institutes of Architects. His designs appeared in textbooks today across the country. The local historical society was proud of this fact, and rightly so. And, of course, it *was* a fine-looking house. Taryn was immediately in love with it, the same way she fell in love with most older homes that were in disrepair and needed a little love, despite the bad feelings she'd had when she'd first turned down the drive.

Unfortunately, although the house was solid and, in her mind, easily fixable (all old buildings were worth preserving in Taryn's mind), a couple of rooms on the front had collapsed years ago, and now lay in a rumpled heap on the sunny grass.

Parking her old Dodge in front, she got out with her Nikon (affectionately named Miss Dixie) slung over her shoulder and began walking around, taking shots when it suited her. She was paid to paint, but she always started with photographs of her subject. Not only did they help jog her memory later, but it was also how she got to know her surroundings. She had a special relationship with her camera and through the viewfinder, she saw architectural details she might otherwise miss. Miss Dixie was often her eyes and picked up on things that Taryn herself sometimes missed. They were a team.

Goosebumps dotted her arms and thighs as she walked through the grass. As she'd sprained her ankle once in a gopher hole while walking backward trying to get a shot of a gable, she was now mindful of any critters or mole holes that might be lurking. She knew she needed to pull herself together. The initial feeling she got upon pulling into the driveway was waning and she tried hard to ignore it further. Her connection with the properties she worked with was both her strongest asset and her weakest link. She felt for old houses and buildings the way many people felt for animals and children. In some ways, the old houses she became attached to *were* her children, or at least her foster kids for a little while. Taryn didn't understand how anyone couldn't love these remnants from the past with their heartbreaking beauty and grace. And when they were abandoned and neglected, they were almost even more beautiful to her. They all had pasts and stories to her; sometimes, she let herself become close to them before she even got to know them. For someone who wasn't much of a romantic when it came to men, she had no qualms when it came to love at first sight with buildings.

For whatever reason, this house and farm tugged at her through the photographs the Stokes County Historical Society sent her before she'd even had the chance to see it in person. Now, seeing it in person and finding it sadly neglected, this beautiful farm had taken her a little by surprise. And it *had* been a long drive up from Tennessee. That could be the only plausible explanation for the sudden emotions she'd experienced when she'd entered the property.

She hoped.

Taryn didn't spook easily but she did pick up on the past. It's what made her good at her job: the ability to empathize with her subjects. *It's not real death you're sensing*, she told herself as she walked around, *it's the death of this grand house.*

It didn't matter that she'd only been commissioned to paint the front of the house: She would take photos inside and out of the entire thing. She'd even spend time photographing the surrounding farm and outbuildings. Taryn believed that to paint anything, you must know it completely. Although the back door might not be in her finished painting, it didn't mean it wasn't important. She had to understand how it fit into the overall structure. Her degree in Historical Preservation taught her that everything about the building (and in this case, the entire farm) was important.

Her degree in Art helped taught her appreciation of the details. Her own sense of curiosity and adventure filled in the rest.

The owner, Reagan Jones, would meet her there tomorrow and show her around, but she'd had a hankering to get on the road and arrived a day earlier than expected, wanting to see it for herself. She worked best without an audience.

The scent was still there, prickling the edge of her mind, but she ignored it. It would come and go but learning to push it down was something she'd perfected over the years. She wasn't there to talk or think about death; she was there to bring a moment of the past to life again.

The house appeared to be structurally sound as far as she could tell. She'd worked with enough architects to know what to look for, and a quick tour of the cellar didn't give any indication that the floors might collapse under her should she decide to walk around upstairs. However, the wolf spiders down there were more than enough to satisfy her curiosity of *that* particular part of the house. (She didn't really do spiders, either.)

It wasn't the most beautiful house she'd ever seen, but the stone frame made it visually interesting and the fluttering torn curtains on the second floor made her sad. The worst part of her job was in knowing that many of the structures she painted would be demolished and gone soon after she left, but it gave her solace to know at least someone cared enough to document their existence. Without that, she wouldn't have a job.

A stroll around the back showed her the addition; a jolting white plank work that she was sure embarrassed the original home. She imagined buildings had memories and feelings and held onto them the same way people did, although this wasn't something she normally shared with people she didn't know (or most she *did)*. Most people might find this romanticism a little nutty. She had just turned thirty, but she'd learned a long time ago that not everyone shared her sentiments when it came to inanimate objects.

Strangely enough, considering the fact the front doors were so tightly bound, the back door was standing wide open. The screen door had fallen off its hinges and lay across the grass where dandelions grew through the tears and holes. She could see all the way into what appeared to be a darkened kitchen and through the small window on the other side of the room, which was not boarded up like the other windows.

She stood there on the wooden steps, a little rotted through but they still held her, and weighed her options. Should she invite herself in? After all, she was hired to do a job here, although, to be fair, it wasn't by the owner himself but by the Stokes County Historical Society. (She figured they must've come into some grant money to afford her fees.)

She wasn't exactly a stranger when it came to inviting herself into empty, deserted places. She'd been known to scale a fence or two and climbing into windows of abandoned houses was not unheard of back when she was younger and nimbler. But she wasn't the spring chicken she once was and here she felt as though there were eyes on her, watching each move she made and the feeling was an uncomfortable one. A quick look around revealed hers was the only vehicle for as far as she could see, but Taryn nevertheless got the feeling she wasn't alone.

However, the sense of adventure finally won out.

Figuring that asking for forgiveness was always easier than asking for permission, she decided to give it a go and continue her exploration. Gently, she stepped up onto the cracked cement landing and peered into the darkened doorway. A peek into the shadowy room confirmed that it was a kitchen. An old tin coffee pot still set on the ancient stove and a round table was covered by a plastic red checkered table cloth that was starting to mildew. There were bird and rodent droppings all over it, and most of it was black but the pattern was still visible through the stains and debris. Some tin cans littered the table and counters, as if someone had recently walked away from them.

"Hello!" she called into the house. She was met with silence.

Taking a chance, she crossed over the frame and entered the house.

Despite the warm summer morning, the house was cool; almost cold. The sense that she was an intruder was amplified by the objects that littered the room. The plates, the utensils, the tablecloth, the coffee pot—it was as if someone had just gotten up and left. That is, if they had left twenty years ago or more.

A small door led from the kitchen into what she assumed was a dining room and she walked toward it, her ears tuned into the sounds of the house. She heard nothing. The dining room held an old metal table but was otherwise bare, save for a couple of empty boxes and some dated calendars on the wall. A living room awaited her on the other side. She stopped in the door frame and held her breath, listening. She had grown accustomed to working alone in deserted places and was usually able to tell whether anyone was nearby simply by listening and taking stock of her surroundings. Sometimes, the simple change of air currents was enough. This time, the house was deathly still. Exhaling deeply, she continued into the living room.

The moment she crossed the door, she held her breath again, but this time subconsciously. Second by second, the air thickened around her, a feeling of pressure increased on her chest and back, and cold chills raced down her shoulders to her fingertips. Her legs nearly buckled under her from the shock. To steady herself, she placed her left hand on the wall and felt crumbling paper under her fingers. It felt like dead flesh decaying beneath her touch and she quickly snatched her hand away and wiped it on her jeans. "Get a grip, dummy," she mumbled to herself. She was a pro at giving herself pep talks. She might be used to exploring old places, and might have even been used to picking up on scents and energy, but that didn't mean she didn't get scared. She was no fool.

The room was dark, darker than the kitchen. The single pale ray of light that filtered in through the boarded windows revealed a dilapidated couch and a coffee table turned on its end. The rug was old and moth-eaten, with rodent droppings speckling its once green and red design. The furniture was at least forty years old, if she were to guess, at least some of it. Other pieces were even older. The house had been empty for a very, very long time. There was nothing menacing about the room itself or the objects it contained, but the air...the air. It was stifling.

Taryn took another step forward and it hit her again, the wave of power and the horrible scent. Wrapping her arms tightly around herself, an old habit of self-defense, she slowly made her way toward the center of the room. It felt like walking through molasses, every step taking more effort than the last. Moving through the darkness didn't feel real and for a fleeting moment, she wondered if perhaps she had fallen asleep in her car while she was driving and was dreaming. She stood in the center, slowly turning around and around, and saw nothing out of the ordinary. The air was still without even the sound of mice in the walls, and yet she felt as if she'd entered a cyclone. A dull roar started first in her left ear and then in her right and as pressure filled her head she got the overwhelming feeling she was chest deep in water, unable to properly catch her breath.

I'm not wanted here, she thought to herself and the cold air rippled as if her inner voice was heard, and the house was agreeing with her.

Giving into another habit, she quickly turned on Miss Dixie and began snapping pictures around the room. The brief flashes of light were soothing and the sound of the shutter hypnotic. She always felt less alone when her camera was on. It had become a friend over the years, so much so that she continued to get it fixed rather than purchase a new one. The pressure slowly eased off her chest and back and the roar stopped as the camera clicked and flashed. Soon, it was just a gloomy living room again.

Gathering new courage again with her camera on, she decided against making a run for the back door. That didn't mean she didn't head for it at a quick pace, however. Another room was visible through the doorway in front of her and there were two staircases on either side of the room that she assumed led to bedrooms, but instead of continuing, she turned and went back to the kitchen, snapping pictures as she went. The moment she stepped into the brighter light, the feeling of coldness left her, as did the dread.

Back outside, Taryn let out a huge exhale and a nervous laugh as she turned and faced the house again. "What the *hell* was what?" she asked aloud, accusingly, as she glared at the stone walls.

Sighing, Taryn returned to her car, this time with a quicker step. For once, she was afraid she might have encountered a house that wasn't particularly pleased at her presence. She was going to have to win it over.

. . .

Taryn checked into her hotel room, a nondescript chain with five stories that looked like every other place she'd ever stayed in and went through her file on the house on Snowden Lane. Windwood Farm, it had been called, and that's what she aimed to title her painting and call it from here on out.

A purposeless reality show on VH-1 (her biggest vice, although not her only one) played softly in the background, mostly for company. She knew it might cost her some brain cells, but it somehow mollified her to see rock stars she had once idolized stooping to the level of looking for dates on television. Everyone was apparently going through a dry spell.

What she'd felt at the house unnerved her. Okay, who was she fooling, it had *scared* her. But she didn't have the luxury of giving into those fears. Last month, her car broke down and she'd needed a new transmission. Between that and some dental work back in the spring, her meager savings were cleared out. Lots of offers had come through, but they just barely covered the bills. Taryn was in financial trouble, hardly able to do more than make her credit card payments and rent. Everyone wanted her; nobody wanted to pay much. She *needed* this job. Without it, she might end up on the street. Whatever was in the house would learn to live with the fact that they were going to be stuck together for the next month or so. Besides, she didn't really believe in ghosts and bad vibes couldn't kill her.

She didn't have much history on the place other than dates. She knew a little bit about it from her correspondence with the president of the historical society, though. The first owner had the home built and lived there until 1902. The second owner, and the last person to really live there, bought it in 1903 and lived there until 1934. Although the next owner bought it right away and apparently moved furniture in from the looks of things, it was never truly lived in again, although the land was farmed. The house was sold again in the 1970s. The current owner was the son of the last owner. He inherited the house from his father. That was all Taryn knew. For all intents and purposes, despite the addition and the furniture inside, the house had been empty since 1934 according to her correspondence.

She was curious about what had happened to the house, but Taryn wasn't there to make judgments on the events that occurred during the house's lifespan, at least not out loud. She would probably judge them eventually because, well, she was human. In Taryn's occupation, it was more important that she painted the structures she saw as they would have been in their glory days, before the devastation they were currently facing. She was to see through their destruction and find remnants of their former splendor and life and try to capture that in paint for future preservation. Before they were demolished. Or, in some rare cases, to help with their restoration. It was true, anyone could go in and snap pictures of their house or property, even the owners themselves, but what *she* offered was something special.

Taryn's talent was in seeing things and places the way they once were and then showing that in her paintings through creativity and a certain amount of sensitivity. Her degree and studies of historical architecture helped her look at even the most dilapidated of places and restructure them in her paintings, sometimes the only complete version of the building her clients had ever seen. She'd been called in to paint houses that had little more than the columns still standing, and she'd been able to give the clients beautiful (their word, not hers, she wasn't *that* narcissistic) renderings of their ancestral homes complete with second floor, attic, and gazebo.

It was true, of course, that most of the places she was hired to capture were in shambles, which made her job a lot harder. This one, however, still looked secure from the outside. Painting it would take a little imagination on her part, since part of it had crumbled, although she had a feeling she would still need to use sensitivity.

Sometimes that sensitivity could get her in trouble. It was one thing to use your imagination to visualize the way a grand staircase used to look with its polished oak and sparkling crystal chandelier above it. It was another thing to actually *see* it. And sometimes, just sometimes, she thought she could. If she closed her eyes hard enough, she imagined and even *saw* what the place would have looked like before time and neglect set in. She even dreamed about the places she worked in, sometimes seeing them fully furnished and ready for balls or weddings or decorated for the holidays.

Occasionally, she became so wrapped up in a place she became attached to it and invested in it, and sometimes it was hard to move away from those feelings once the job ended. She'd become part of more than one house. It was an occupational hazard. Of course, she wanted to purchase every single one she fell in love with. But nobody paid her that well.

Two

Reagan Jones was an energetic young man, no more than thirty, with a developer's eye and a politician's smile. Taryn had met many men like him over the years, those who thirsted for real estate development and hated to see an empty field as much as some people hated to see strip malls. This was the first time she'd met one quite so young, however.

He hopped out of his SUV with a big smile and had her walking around the property again in no time, pointing out landmarks and explaining his plans for the area. "It's all going to be a subdivision," he said hurriedly. "But not one of those with all the houses looking the same. Each house will have at least one acre, maybe two if they want to purchase more. It will be like having a mini farm!"

It wouldn't be anything *like having a mini farm*, Taryn thought to herself, but she smiled pleasantly. He was, for the time being, sort of her boss. "I'm going to have to get a little more information about the property and was hoping you could answer some questions for me."

"Well, I can surely try," he said seriously, his large hazel eyes growing wide. He had a slight paunch and some of his features were a little large for his small face, but he wasn't an unattractive man and Taryn was receiving a warm vibe from him, despite his enthusiasm for tearing down a large, seemingly structurally sound, and beautiful home. He spoke with an easy drawl but even with his polished look and laid-back style (he wore loafers and jeans) he was calculating. She suspected that he was one of those men whom everyone liked, even when they were being bulldozed. "I don't rightly know a whole lot about it. It belonged to my daddy who bought it from the third owner. It got passed down to me because I'm an only child. My daddy owned a lot of properties around here. Nobody's lived in it since the thirties. My daddy was the oldest son, his other brothers died in the war, and he lived there on the property for about a year and then gave it up. Lived in a camper. Never used the house at all. Just storage, mostly. After he built our house he just used the barn here. The other owners before him didn't really live in it at all. Maybe a few nights here and there. Nobody's lived in it permanently, as far as I know, since 1934."

"It looks like it," Taryn mumbled. "I'm sorry, but I stopped here yesterday and walked around a bit. I went inside because it was open and for a minute I was startled and thought someone might be staying here. It looks lived in."

"Yeah," Reagan laughed. "It does that to you. Me? I don't like going in there unless I have to. My wife won't go in at all. Says it gives her the willies. Local kids don't even bother it. You won't find anyone sneaking in there to smoke or fool around. I could leave the door open year-round and not a soul would touch it."

Taryn must have looked skeptical because he laughed. "What? You don't believe in ghosts? And I thought your job was seeing things that aren't there. Isn't that another way of seeing ghosts?"

Taryn shrugged. "I chalk it up to having a good imagination. And no, I've never seen a ghost. I don't think I believe in them. Not really."

Reagan laughed and patted her shoulder. "Well, maybe that's why you haven't seen them."

"I think I believe in something," Taryn smiled. "I just don't know what yet."

"Stick around," Reagan laughed. "Just stick around. You will!"

Considering her occupation, people were always asking her if she ever saw any ghosts. But what could she tell them? That she always felt the presence of something but could never quite put her finger on what it was? She liked to think of her talent as a kind of sensitivity to leftover energy. Like the photographs she took, Taryn thought places held memories and figured she was tuned into those, or something to that effect. Occasionally, she did stumble across a spooky place that made her feel uncomfortable, like the old mental hospital in Danvers, Massachusetts (or that Victorian monstrosity that had her seeing shadows and questioning her sanity a few times), but usually after being in it for a couple of days she could get past whatever she felt and work well within the environment. If she remembered that what she was seeing and feeling was nothing more than a memory or hologram, she kept the ill feelings at bay.

Yesterday had been unnerving, and she hadn't slept well the night before, but new places always did that to her. Besides, it was possible that she had simply been tired and had imagined what she felt. Old houses had personalities and perhaps this one's was just a little strong. It didn't mean that she slept any easier that night, however.

After a quick trip around the exterior of the house, Reagan went back to the kitchen door Taryn had entered the day before. "This is about the only way you can get in and out. Front's all boarded up. I can take the boards down if it will help with the doors and stuff."

"It would help, actually, especially if the original door is still there behind the planks. Why do you have them boarded up if you say people won't come in here?"

"Well, when I first got the house, I didn't know that. Had the whole thing boarded up. When I saw nobody was going to bother it, I took them down in the back. I like to come in and check on things from time to time...not often though," he added.

The kitchen looked the same, vacant and unused, but was set for a breakfast scene that was never going to happen. On closer inspection, the tin cans had obviously been there for a long time, possibly twenty years or more.

Reagan took her into a room off the kitchen she hadn't seen the day before. It was a small, narrow room with a single bed and a battered dresser. Both were in bad shape. A man's work clothes were scattered about the floor and hangers were tossed carelessly about. It appeared someone left in a hurry. The clothes didn't give the impression to be that far out of style, and Taryn looked at them in confusion. "Was somebody staying here?"

"Yeah. Two summers ago, we decided to fix this place up, me and my wife. Thought we could add on to it, it doesn't have but two bedrooms upstairs and we've got three kids, and make it real nice again. I heard it used to be a real beauty. So, we brought this guy in to pack up the good stuff and haul out the junk. Do some of the landscaping, too. Told him he could stay here while he did it, cause we knew it would take a couple of months.

"Well, he stays for about a week and then ups and leaves. Tacks a note on my front door saying that he can't stay no more and he's gotta be getting back to Indiana, to home. So, I call him and ask him if he wants me to send him his clothes and such that he left behind and he says no, he don't need a thing. Beat all I ever seen."

Reagan shook his head at the memory and laughed. "I came in here and looked around and found his wallet, full of money. I mailed that to him. Must've been in a hurry. I'm gonna put in a call to the Salvation Army and see if they can use any of this furniture. My wife has everything at home the way she wants it and doesn't want me bringing anything else in to mess it up."

Taryn smiled pleasantly and gave a nod, hoping it looked to be in encouragement.

The jovial smile never left Reagan's face. "You'll understand that better if you ever meet the missus. She's real particular about certain things."

"If there are two bedrooms upstairs, why didn't he sleep up there?"

Reagan shrugged, and turned back to the kitchen. "Don't know. Might make more sense when you see one of them, though. Came in here that first day and looked around and then said he'd rather sleep down here. I hauled in a bed from our storage unit. He said that was fine."

"So, after that, you decided not to fix it up?"

"No, we still thought we might. My wife came over a few times and worked outside. Still keeps some gardening tools here because the shed here is bigger. We live in a subdivision I developed myself and only have but one outbuilding to make room for the swing set and swimming pool. Came in with some boxes—you'll see them in the living room—and tried to pack up some stuff herself. Then she said she didn't like it anymore and wasn't going to come back by herself. She got spooked. That was the end of that."

They were heading toward the living room, and her breath caught. She hoped that whatever she felt before was nothing but the result of a long day of driving because she was damned if she was going to look like a fool in front of him. The scent that accosted her on her first visit was already less potent than before. But when they stepped across the doorway, she was still surprised. Nothing. Not even a chill passed over her skin. *Maybe it had just been an illusion*, she told herself.

"This here was the dining room," Reagan continued. "My daddy was going to use it as a living area himself. Must've been easier to heat than the living room and the parlor. I don't know. There was an old couch in here. We already hauled it away."

"Was he related to the other owner? Your dad, I mean?"

"Oh, no. He bought it at auction. And that guy did, too. None of us knew Robert Bowen, the one who lived here longest."

"Did Robert live here alone?" The personal background was probably more helpful to Taryn than any other research she could have done. Sure, she had her design books back in her room and a history of the area, but it was the people who made the house and figuring out how they lived put it all into perspective.

Reagan shook his head and went on into the adjoining room. "No. Well, at the end he did. Died of a heart attack or something or other. In the beginning, he was married. She died around five years into the marriage. One of those old-timey diseases that nobody gets anymore. I can't remember what it's called. Sorry. Don't know much about her. They had a daughter but she died, too. That I do know. After that, he lived alone."

"How did he make his money? And what did he do through the Depression? Or was this area not hit very hard?"

"Oh, this area was hit. Kentucky was hit just as hard as anyplace else, though the smaller towns didn't get all of them riots and stuff cause they was fairly small to begin with and employment had always been bad around here. But it got hit. No, he made his money from tobacco, same as a lot of people here. Even in a Depression, people gotta smoke."

So he was a farmer, Taryn made a mental note. And this wasn't a grand house inside, although it was large, so he probably did at least some of the work himself. She wondered when the wife and daughter died. Local records would show that, if she decided it was important enough to know. It might not be. She had a lot to work with already. She was already starting to get to know the house and too much more might muddle things up. But sometimes her curiosity got the best of her. It was funny how stepping through the doors of a place could instantly start her wheels turning.

The living room was large as well. She hadn't noticed before. She'd been too caught up in trying to figure out what was going on. It was the front room, and a glance at the boarded-up door gave Taryn faint chills. She brushed them off by telling herself the boards simply blocked out the natural light and made the room unusually dark. That was enough to give anyone the creeps.

Reagan, as if reading her mind, chuckled. "Guess it does make the place spooky. Sorry it's so dark in here. I'll get those taken down. Won't be able to take any pictures if you can barely see your hand in front of your face. I read your website. I know you like to take pictures first," he said at her bemused expression.

"That's okay," she shrugged. "I don't mind being cyber stalked."

"This here was the living room. Nothing left in here anymore except the fireplaces. And some old furniture, of course. When Dad died, we took most of the good furniture, especially from these front rooms. Sold anything we could. Nothing really in here, though. Never was. Seems like that's as far as they got though because as you saw from the kitchen and as you'll see from the upstairs, everything's still left up there from when Robert and his family lived here in the 20s and 30s. Interesting thing about this room is the two staircases. See?"

Taryn looked around and indeed, saw the two sturdy wooden staircases in the two corners of the room. "Where do they go?"

"One goes up to one bedroom and one goes to the other. Oddest thing I've ever seen. You'd think maybe they was added separately but they weren't. House was built at the same time except for the back. After the Bowens died off, nobody ever really used the place. Not for long anyway. Just farmed the land."

Taryn nodded absently and then wandered over to the nearest staircase and studied it. It was simple and sturdy, but not ornate. Something one might find in a farmhouse. A ray of pale light fell down the steps, suggesting there might be a window upstairs. The fireplace mantel *was* decorative, however, with carvings and decorations adorning it. Why spend money on one and not the other?

Taryn was so intent on her musings she didn't notice when Reagan wandered out of one room and into the next. Suddenly, a wave of cold air blasted her and she staggered, caught off-guard. Cold needles pricked her skin and as she brought her arms up to cross in front of her protectively, the room began to swim. As if seeing it through a wave of water, she blinked her eyes, and watched as murky shadows began to manifest. Scared at first, she couldn't help but be a little intrigued as well, and she experimentally reached out her hand to touch a nearby passing shape. As her fingers made contact, a flash of lightning struck them. "Ouch!" she cried out in pain.

"You okay in there?" Reagan's voice was faint, as if coming from a well, with a slight echo. She could hear his footsteps coming toward her and she closed her eyes again. When she opened them, he was standing before her and the room was once again empty.

"Sorry, splinter," she tried to laugh. "From the staircase."

A puzzled look flickered across his face and then it was gone. "You gotta be careful in here," he shrugged. "This place is falling apart, and you don't know what all you can get into. The floor's sound as a rock but I don't keep insurance on it. I should, but I don't. So, don't get hurt and sue me." He flashed her a million-dollar smile and winked. Taryn smiled back.

With shaking legs that belied her outward appearance, Taryn tried to compose herself. *Am I losing my mind?* she asked herself worriedly. *What the hell is going on in here?* Reagan appeared easy and comfortable; an owner simply walking through the rooms of a house he had no use for. How was it possible he didn't feel something a little off? Or did he?

The next room, a smaller parlor, was like the front room and boasted a fireplace, this one missing a mantel. Otherwise, the room was dark and bare, with little to distinguish it from any number of empty rooms Taryn had seen in other homes from the same time. The darkness was throwing Taryn off, but she wasn't surprised Reagan had boarded the place up; this was the kind of place that teenagers and rounders liked to use for a party pad, except for the fact that Reagan said he didn't have a problem with that.

"You wanna go upstairs?" His voice echoed and bounced off the walls, a lonely and hollow sound in the darkness.

Taryn nodded, and they began their ascent up the plain staircase. "Do you think anyone was ever going to replace these staircases with something more permanent and just never got around to it?"

Reagan shook his head. "Don't know. Kind of ugly for the house, huh?"

They both laughed.

"Still here though," he added. "So many of these get vandalized and ripped apart. Guess nobody wanted this one. My uncle sold some of the mantels. My daddy runned an antique store for years. People like those old mantels. Them and the bannisters are usually the first things to get ripped out of these old houses. But not this one. Easy to see why."

It was a surprise to find that the stairs opened right into the bedroom. No hallway, no sitting area, nothing. An unusual lack of privacy for the time, Taryn noted, especially since houses built in the mid-nineteenth century were so fond of their doors. It made conserving heat easier since you could always shut off rooms you weren't using but in today's designs, people were all about open concepts and wide-open spaces. Those wide-open spaces sometimes made Taryn feel a little claustrophobic. She liked her doors and actual rooms that had specific purposes.

Mysteriously enough, if the living room and parlor were mostly empty and bare of odds and ends from the past, this room looked as if it had just been abandoned the day before. The paint on the old white wrought iron metal bed might have been peeling and the mattress moldy, but it was pushed to the window where dainty lace curtains still fluttered in the morning breeze. They were moth-eaten and dusty, but still intact except for a few tears here and there. Mildewed sheets were thrown haphazardly across the bed and fell onto the floor, as if someone just recently pushed them aside. A featherbed was smoothed over the frame and a few loose feathers drifted in the air, aroused by the air currents Taryn and Reagan disturbed. A broken rocking chair sat in the corner of the room, staring into the middle of the floor, as if keeping watch.

A lone waterfall dresser was pushed against the far side of the wall and it was to this that Taryn's attention was drawn to the most. The drawers were all gaping, revealing articles of clothing that could have been slips or nightgowns. A small oak jewelry box set atop the dresser and it was open as well, displaying rings, cameos, and necklaces. Some of them, even to Taryn's untrained eye, appeared to be the real deal. A porcelain china doll was lying on its side, its once fine face smashed into pieces. A set of keys rested beside it: heavy, masculine skeleton keys that appeared out of place in the otherwise feminine room. The entire dresser looked as if someone just recently went through it in a hurry, maybe looking for something.

Reagan was watching her, his long arms folded causally across his chest, his polo shirt and jeans looking out of place. Taryn felt as if both were standing amid a movie set. She was confused. "So you say that people don't come in here and go through things?"

"That's right," he replied with a faint smile on his face. He had seen all of this before and was watching her with amusement, waiting for her reaction.

"Well, it looks like someone came in and went through this room," she muttered as she walked over to the dresser and ran her hand over the keys. They were cold and heavy under her fingers.

"Wellll...not exactly. You see, this bedroom has been like this for as long as I can remember."

Taryn turned and looked at him, confused. "What do you mean?"

"It's *always* looked like this. I'm thirty-five years old and it's been this way since I was a baby, probably before. The downstairs? Yeah, kids came and went down there some. But something kept them from going any further. Back in the 70s, my daddy said he ran a few off, some who had taken some silver and things from the dining room. But not in years. My wife, she come up here once and tried to clean. Pushed those drawers closed, put that jewelry back into the box, picked up those papers on the floor, even tried to make the bed. Said that it looking like this all the time bothered her. Then she went back downstairs for a little while. Heard some noises here. When she came back up, it looked just the same as it did before. This room just don't want to be touched."

Three

aryn and Reagan sat on the front steps of the old house, looking out over the fields and gravel lane. "It's in remarkably good condition. I mean, to have been vacant for, what, how many years? Unbelievable." She wasn't sure if she was really going to believe that the house kept people from messing with it, but she was ready to admit there was something special about it.

Reagan nodded. "Part of that is because it's stone. Part of it because we've kept it covered and those old trees right here keep it shaded. I've patched the roof up over the years and there's not a drop of water that can get into the house. It will come into the cellar, of course, and the whole thing smells musty. I'm sure if we knock out some of those walls we're gonna find black mold up to our ears, but it *is* still standing."

Making both physical and mental notes while Reagan talked, now she stopped. "So why do it now? Why tear it down? Why not build around it? Restore it?" It really did break her heart to think of something that had stood there for so long to be knocked over in the name of a subdivision and "progress."

"I don't have the money. People look at me and think I do, but I don't. I borrow it, same as everybody else does. I have debts, too. I had a guy look at it once. He said it would cost as much to fix it as it would to build a new one. The foundation is fair, as far as we know, but you're looking at a house that was built two centuries ago and hasn't been updated since. No plumbing, no electric, weak floors, needs a new roof...It's just not my project. And then there's the other thing...nobody here would want to live in it. Would take an outsider. Fact is, if it wasn't for the Stokes County Historical Society throwing a fit over it, I wouldn't have even called you here to do your thing to it. No offense or nothing," he added hurriedly.

Taryn nodded. That was usually the case—the owners rarely took their own initiative in these matters. She was used to it. But at least Reagan was honest about it. But what had he meant about nobody from there not wanting to live in it?

"Well, I hate to see it go, but then I hate to see all old houses go. It's yours and you can do what you want with it. I can get started this evening," she said as she stood up and dusted off her pants. "I like the sunset light the best, next to early

123

morning. But I'm not really a morning person. Take me about three weeks to finish, maybe a little longer. I'll say five weeks to be on the safe side."

"No worries," Reagan smiled. "We don't plan on doing anything with it until the end of summer. I've got my hands full with some other business as it is. Feel free to poke around and do what you have to do. Just don't get hurt."

"Thanks. I usually spend the first few days just kind of getting acquainted with the place, looking around, doing some sketches and photographs."

Reagan shrugged. "However you have to work. My wife? She's a photographer too. Mostly kids. You do a lot of houses like this?"

"Not so much anymore," Taryn answered quickly. "Mostly museums and historical sites. I don't do a lot of private homes anymore. This one...called to me, I guess you could say. Or else the ladies at the historical society were pretty persistent."

Reagan smiled. "Well, they are that, I can attest."

"I have my cell on me if you need anything," she said as she started toward her car.

"Oh," Reagan called after her. "You won't need it. Can't get a signal out here. The company says there's coverage, but this must be a dead zone."

. . .

When the Stokes County Historical Society first approached Taryn about the job, she was reluctant. She didn't do jobs associated with many private homes anymore. This was for reasons of her own, but mostly because the owners liked to nose around and make her nervous and she enjoyed having free run of the place. It had taken some pleading on their part for her to accept this one, and she did so only after they assured her it was vacant and nobody would bother her. And, of course, once they assured her that they could afford her. She hated to be petty about the money thing, but she really did need it.

It was the name that drew her to the house from the beginning: Windwood. It didn't take much to understand where it came from, either. With the house's position atop the ridge the wind was certainly strong enough to blow you over if you didn't watch your step. She was going to have to weigh her easel down and clamp her canvas to it. Luckily, the tall maple and oak trees blocked the worst of the wind. She assumed there had once been more woods than what were presently visible, but the ones she could see were thick and dark and almost romantic with their position at the foot of the valley.

She'd been in constant contact with the president and secretary of the Stokes County Historical Society for almost six weeks and she knew the time was coming when she'd have to go over and meet the women (and presumably men) who were a part of it, especially since they were technically her employers. But so far, she'd been engrossed with getting acquainted with the house and meeting Reagan, the rightful owner anyway.

They hadn't told her anything about the property itself, just the dates of construction and architectural features she might find interesting. That was enough for her at the time. She'd especially enjoyed the pictures they sent her of the property. Looking back, she'd had no idea that photographs were about to become so important.

The house and surrounding farm certainly appeared ordinary enough in the images they'd sent her; maybe a little sad and forgotten, but those were the kinds of places that drew her.

Taryn started her degree program when she was eighteen, but she'd started her career much earlier. Since Matt first got his license at age sixteen, he had driven them around to deserted houses and buildings so she could "explore" (a nicer word than breaking and entering), and the two of them could have mini adventures. Matt was usually just the chauffeur and sidekick in these excursions; they were really all about Taryn. She'd known Matt for more than twenty years and he'd been humoring her for all of them, even when their first mode of transport had been nothing but their bikes and he'd ridden her around on the handlebars, her pigtails flying in the wind.

At first, she'd carried her 35-mm camera with her everywhere they went and snapped furiously at old barns, gnarled oak trees, and abandoned farmhouses with cracked windows and dilapidated roofs with daffodils growing through sagging porches. For every old house and ancient barn and warehouse they'd discovered, she created stories about the former inhabitants: who'd they been, what they'd seen, how they'd lived and worked. Matt had listened and humored her while her imagination spun tales from the past. She'd hated waiting almost a week for her pictures to be developed back then, but it was exciting, too. She'd had to be much more discriminate with her picture taking back when developing the rolls cost money she didn't really have. She'd made sure every shot was framed to perfection. He'd had such patience with her as she got down on her knees, on her stomach, and even had him boost her up on his shoulders from time to time.

Then, on her fifteenth birthday, her grandmother gave her a Polaroid camera. That made things *really* interesting. Although the quality wasn't as good, she loved having the instantaneous product right in her hand. Sometimes, she took both cameras along with her and snapped until she'd run out of film.

She hadn't discovered her flair for painting until she was in high school. Her choices for an elective were between art and shop and even though she loved architecture, she was terrible at woodworking (her parents mistook her 4-H birdhouse for a sailboat), so art it was. Her teacher was tolerant and understanding and helped her to develop a skill she didn't even know she'd possessed.

The first building she had reconstructed in a painting was a barn. She loved barns, especially the ones that were used for tobacco because they had all the "little doors" as she'd called them when she was a kid. This barn was falling in, but still boasted brilliant red paint that shone in the sun and it also had a glorious cupola, something she almost never saw. Using her imagination and other barns of similar design for inspiration, she painted it as though it was in its former glory. The painting won her a prize at a regional art contest for high school students and the hobby of painting dilapidated buildings as they had once been took place.

When she was eighteen, she volunteered as a docent at a local historical home for the summer. During the eighteenth and nineteenth centuries, slave quarters existed on the grounds. Only half of one of the buildings still stood, although the sites of the others were marked. After gaining permission from the director, she spent a good part of her free time that summer reading through the letters, journals, and other documentation that were kept on hand at the museum from the family members and guests of the home during the time. She also spent a lot of time at Vanderbilt University's research library. Within three months, Taryn could create a painting of the grounds, including an eerily accurate representation of the mansion and all the outbuildings, and the former slave quarters and a grist mill that was also in ruins. The painting still hung in the front hall of the museum. And it helped her eventually win a scholarship.

She wasn't entirely sure she believed Reagan's story about the dresser and the bedroom. She admitted there was something off about the house, but, *really*, a house that didn't want anybody to touch anything in it? Or rather—a room that didn't want anyone to touch anything in it? Not that she blamed the poor woman, of course. She didn't like her things bothered, either.

True, she felt something in the house. She wasn't going to deny that. And there was some kind of interesting sensation on the property she couldn't put her finger on. But she had felt that before. And, true, she wasn't sure she felt welcome there. But she had also felt that before. Of course, her vision *had* wavered in the living room. But maybe she could explain that, as well. She was tired, unfocused. It was hot outside, muggy. The air was old and musty. Who knew what kind of mold was inside those walls. She loved old buildings more than most people, but black mold was serious business and could do funny things to people and it didn't take much of it to make you crazy.

There was always an explanation for the weird things that happened in old houses and she tried not to get too excited and jump to ghosts right away.

Besides, if anyone had a reason to want to believe in ghosts, it was her.

. . .

Dressed in cutoff jeans, an old Eagles T-shirt, and sneakers, Taryn headed back out to Windwood Farm in plenty of time to catch the evening light. She didn't bring her paints with her on this trip because she first liked to sketch what she would later put paintbrush to. She'd go over that sketch nearly a dozen times before she was happy with it. And frankly, she would never really be completely satisfied with it. She'd even go over it in her dreams. The photographs she took would help. She hadn't uploaded the previous ones to her laptop yet, but she would that evening.

The weight of the day was starting to take its toll on her. She was still a little tired from the drive up. It had been three years since she'd worked at a private residence, even a deserted one, and the last one was a little bit of a disaster. The owner watched her like a hawk and made her a nervous wreck and she'd still been recovering from a difficult time in her life. The painting wasn't her best, even though her client, the Arts Council, was pleased with it. It was the longest month of her life.

Taryn spent the afternoon driving around town, checking out Vidalia's center and some of the local historical sites. There weren't many, but the town tried. They seemed to be particularly proud of their railroad and their depot was restored, offering visitors a small museum with relics from the Great Depression and mid-century that were especially interesting. Unfortunately, like many small towns in the south, urban sprawl paved the way for strip malls and big shoebox stores and Main Street was dead or on its way out. There had once been some charm to the town with its turn-of-the-century courthouse and wide, tree-lined streets but much of that was lost when pitted against the heavy traffic flow, the vacant storefronts, and the flashing neon billboards.

She drove up on a ridge that overlooked the valley and was startled to see several housing developments full of identical structures, all with the same roofs and fences. They looked like dominoes from where she sat in her car. She'd heard from construction friends of hers that the new houses weren't built nearly as strong as the old ones, so she wouldn't be surprised if a strong push really would topple them over one by one.

Parking her car in the middle of the driveway, she hopped out and grabbed her canvas bag filled with her sketchpad and charcoals and started toward the middle of the wide, flat yard. The curtains fluttering in the breeze on the second floor caught her attention. Because she was looking up at the movement, she didn't notice the stone jutting out of the ground, and suddenly found herself on her face.

"Shit!" she screamed. Her ankle twisted painfully under her as her bag landed a few feet away. Turning over, she looked back at the culprit. A large creek stone was stuck in the ground behind her at an incredibly awkward angle, its sharp edge pointing up into the sky. "Good thing I didn't fall on it," she muttered to herself, imagining blood squirting from her head and not being discovered for days as she slowly bled to death from a head wound (she was nothing if not dramatic).

Crawling over to the rock, she inspected it more closely. There were several others around it, making a complete circle. On closer inspection, it appeared to encircle a hole that had been filled in. She hoped whoever had done it had filled in well and with more than just loose dirt. She wasn't keen on the idea of falling into a century old abyss and left alone for several days...if she was ever discovered at all. She didn't do well with dark, hollow places.

"Hope it's not a sinkhole," she sighed. It wasn't unusual for her to talk to herself. She always worked alone and sometimes she got tired of the quietness. Recently, she'd tried working with an assistant and it had made her nervous. Sometimes, though, she missed having noise. Talking inside her head made her feel crazy but talking aloud made her feel eccentric in a nice kind of way.

Within a few minutes, she was able to quickly make a few sketches of the front of the house, including the maple and oak trees that filled the front yard and the winding driveway that wound its way back to the barns. She paid careful attention to the quivering curtains and boarded up door and windows and after finishing with the charcoal put her sketchpad away and pulled out her Nikon. "Okay, Miss Dixie. It's your turn. Do your thing."

The light was almost faded by then, but she still had more than enough time to walk around the perimeter and do some sunset shots before getting back in the car and grabbing some dinner before going back to the hotel for the night. She would focus on one area of the house at a time as she painted but when she photographed, she liked to catch as many angles as possible.

It really *was* a beautiful area. Although she preferred the mountains to the east and even the flat, sultry thick deltas of the south, these manicured green valleys had their own gentle beauty that was hard to deny. She began to imagine what they must have looked like even half a century ago when the fields were full of tobacco and corn and the air was still and quiet.

She'd once been commissioned to paint an isolated cabin in West Virginia. It was located nearly twenty-five miles off the interstate. It was located so far off the main road that she'd ended up camping out up there the entire two weeks it took to get the job done. Amazed at how quiet the air had been without the sound of airplanes and cars around her, the stillness was both soothing and unsettling. She'd needed that at the time, even if she hadn't known it at the time. She didn't have cell phone service, television, or internet service the whole time she'd been up there, so she'd relied on her battery-powered CD player and the stack of CDs she'd brought with her. It was a bit like going through detox. By the time Taryn was finished, she'd lost all track of what was going on in the rest of the world and she'd emerged as though she'd been living in a cocoon.

The "magic hour" wasn't so much an hour as it was a fleeting few minutes and she used every second to her advantage, snapping pictures left and right as she bent, stretched, and stooped, straining to get every angle of the house and property that was humanly possible (and then a few more). Her phone beeped furiously, a reminder she had missed her pre-planned phone call from Matt, but she ignored it. She couldn't call him back now. He would understand.

So used to framing the images she wanted, Taryn barely took the time to even glance in the viewfinder before she moved on to the next image that caught her eye. She never checked her LCD screen while she was taking shots. She considered it bad luck. She and Miss Dixie shared a special rhythm and understood one another.

Taryn took the images that called to her. Every house and property spoke to her in a different way. Sometimes it was the yard. Sometimes it was a house's view. Sometimes it was a house's porch and the way it framed the world in front of it. There was no doubt about it, though. For Windwood Farm, it was the windows to the house that contained its soul. Even the ones that were boarded up and should have been emotionless called to her in ways that were inescapable. Without realizing it, she had soon taken hundreds of shots and nearly used up her memory card as the last rays of sunlight fell into the darkening sky.

Gathering up the remainder of her equipment, she tossed her canvas bag back into her car and turned around in the driveway. Again, she felt the unnerving feel of eyes on the back of her head as she deliberately drove down the gravel toward the gate. Her cell phone gave off its steady beat, the pale light flashing a radiant green into the car's dark interior. The faint smell of death clung to her clothes, prickling at her skin.

. . .

"Oh, honey, we're just so glad you made it there okay!"

The woman on the other end of the line possessed the rough, whiskey-voiced sound older women tend to get after years of smoking. At first, Taryn thought she was talking to a man but then when the voice went into a coughing fit and Taryn heard the rattling sound in the back of her throat, she put it together.

"I made it here without any problems," Taryn agreed. "Found it just fine."

"Well, listen, I'm Priscilla and I'm the secretary for the Stokes County Historical Society. We've talked through email of course, but I thought you deserved a call now that you're here. I'm so sorry we weren't there to meet you but one of our members is in the hospital with pneumonia and we've all just been beside ourselves checking on her and taking care of her house. We've been running around like chickens with our heads cut off!" With that, the woman went into another coughing fit that concerned Taryn a great deal. She waited until she was finished before she spoke.

"That's okay. I'm fine. I went out there today and got started. It's a beautiful place," she added. Taryn was a little forlorn that her baked potato and soup were getting cold while she was having this conversation, but she really couldn't put it off. The woman had already called her three times that day. She'd ignored those calls because she was busy. (Once she was driving, once she'd been in the bathtub, and the third time she'd been having a self-imposed time-out.)

"Oh yes, I knew you'd like it. It's a wonderful farm. Such a shame what's going to happen to it, isn't it? Of course, none of us remember what it used to look like, but you should have seen the farm on the other side of it, too. Now that was something to see! The house was one of the grandest in Kentucky. It was torn down years ago, though," Priscilla said sadly.

"Oh, what happened?" Taryn asked, both out of politeness and interest.

"A tornado took most of it and then it became dangerous. The family had the rest demolished and then they put in one of those subdivisions. It was a real southern beauty, though. The family, the Fitzgerald's, they owned most of the county at the time," Priscilla added.

"Wish I could have seen it," Taryn said sincerely.

"Well, listen, I'll let you get back to your dinner. I just wanted to let you know that we're grateful you're here and that we will see you soon!" As Priscilla hung up the phone, Taryn could hear her coughing again.

The coffee shop soup and baked potato were mostly warm by the time she got to them and the sweet tea felt nice after a long day out in the sun. She'd bought herself a pitcher and some packets at the store and was planning on making her own and taking it out to the farm with her while she worked. Her New Year's resolution included cutting down on caffeine. Normally, she tried not to unleash a decaffeinated version of herself on humanity, but she was really trying to get healthier these days.

. . .

"I wasn't even thinking when I called you earlier. It was just about dusk, wasn't it?" Matt apologized.

Taryn could hear him clanging on metal in the background. He was either cooking or thinking about cooking when she talked to him. They almost always put one another on speakerphone when they talked to each other. She wasn't offended. Neither one could sit still for long periods of time. They had to be doing something. She was currently in a partial stage of undressing herself and had her shirt over her head while she attempted to give him a muffled reply. "Hmuuhyphh..."

"Did you get anything accomplished today?"

Having tugged on her nightgown, she plugged in her flash drive and sat down in front of her computer in the middle of her hotel bed and began uploading her pictures. It was an old laptop and she wasn't optimistic that it was going to be a quick process. It never was. In the meantime, she fell back on the pillow and began flipping through the limited television channels.

"I think so. It's an interesting one. Lots of stone. Bad feelings, you know?"

"Already? That's fast. Hold on just a minute. I'm boiling over..."

Matt loved to cook more than he loved to do just about anything. As a physicist, cooking was his stress reliever, and it was a sad irony he didn't have anyone special in his life to share any of the grand meals he concocted. Often, he tossed out all of the gourmet meal he created night after night. She did appreciate hearing about them, though. "So, what are we having tonight?"

"Nothing special. Just some gumbo. I was feeling New Orleans. It's been stewing all day though. It smells so good. I also made some rosemary ciabatta to go with it. The whole house smells nice and toasty."

"Nice! I had Taco Bell for lunch. And to make it a little classier, I also stopped at Panera Bread and finished it off with a chocolate chip bagel."

Matt sighed. "You're going to die of food poisoning."

"Probably." She didn't tell him what she really had because she was afraid it would ruin her reputation.

A glance at the computer screen showed her the images were loading unreasonably slow this evening, although a few had already popped up. Oh well. There wasn't anything she could do to hurry them along.

"Do you want to hear about the house?" she asked. She knew he wouldn't ask on his own accord. Matt wouldn't think to. He was a little cerebral. Always trapped in his own head.

"Okay. But first, the bad feelings? Are they about the house or are they because...."?

"I think it's the house, Matt. I don't think it's me this time," she answered shortly, a little annoyed.

"Are you sure?" he asked gently. "Because sometimes you can get the two confused. It's not easy working alone when you're in a place like that."

Trying to remember he was just being helpful, she closed her eyes and thought of all the times he had been supportive of her. "I know that sometimes I fall apart a little bit, but it's not like that. This is different. It's the house. Do you want to hear about it or not?"

"I do, I'm sorry. Go ahead."

"Okay...I can see why the Stokes County Historical Society is interested, even without the Governor part. The stonework is beautiful. The property is beautiful. I think the owner is doing a big disservice to someone. Instead of putting in a subdivision, if he doesn't want to renovate, then he could at least just build another house there and take advantage of that nice yard and those views. You're not going to get that with all those houses crammed in there."

Matt sighed. "Oooh! Did I mention that I got to give a tour of the lab today? We had visitors come down from DC! They were very impressed with..."

Taryn managed to tune him out after a few seconds. She (mostly) loved talking to Matt. He was her oldest friend and had stuck with her since childhood. He also understood her like few people did and his house provided refuge when she was feeling stressed and needed a break from the rest of the world, like she often did. There had even been a few times in the past when they tried to kindle a romance between them and sometimes it even worked, at least for small periods of time. But she could only handle him in small doses.

Between "The Golden Girls" on television and making the appropriate noises to Matt on the telephone to let him know she was indeed still listening to him speak, she almost forgot to check on her laptop and her pictures. She was just about to head to the small hotel-sized refrigerator to grab a drink when something caught her eye, and nearly made her topple onto the floor. "What the hell," she muttered, dropping the cell to the floor.

"Taryn?" came Matt's muffled response, sounding a mile away. "You okay?"

Grabbing the computer, she pulled it closer to her and began tapping some buttons, trying to make sense out of what she was seeing. Three, four, five, six...no, FIFTEEN of the eighteen photographs she'd taken of the downstairs rooms were unlike anything she had ever seen before.

When she'd taken them, the rooms were a little dark. They'd contained some furniture, but the furniture was dated, mismatched items from different time periods. Old calendars dotted some of the walls. Boxes lined the floors in two of the rooms. Stains were on the hardwood. The rooms had general unlived in feels to them. The windows were boarded up. The rooms were dark. They'd used flashlights to walk around and see.

But in her pictures...

The boards were gone. In their place were curtains; light, airy, lacy things that let in sunbeams that played across the floors. There was a settee in the parlor. Framed pictures were on the wall. There were no stains. There were no calendars on the walls.

The photographs were not focused. They weren't perfect. The lines were blurry and appeared to be superimposed atop the original ones, perhaps? But it was clear the rooms were the same, only they looked completely different. A glance through the rest of the pictures of the house showed her that none of them had come out. They were all black.

Picking the phone back up, she told an impatient Matt that she'd have to call him back. "Something came up," she explained in a whisper. "I'll tell you later."

. . .

For the next three hours, Taryn alternated between staring at her pictures, cleaning poor Miss Dixie, and poring over the internet. It wasn't helpful. What she was supposed to type into Google, after all? Every time she tried to enter something into the search engine like "things in picture that aren't supposed to be there" the only thing she came up with were pages about camera defects. She was clearly in over her head as far as the paranormal pages went, too. She'd always been sensitive when it came to sappy commercials and cute babies. Since Andrew's accident, she thought she often picked up on some things that maybe other people didn't, but wasn't this taking things just a little bit *too* far?

Still...a small part of her couldn't contain its excitement. She couldn't stop looking at the pictures. It was addictive! Once she got past the shock, she'd hooked up her printer and printed out two copies of every photo she'd taken and then got to work painting them, just in case something happened to the prints themselves. What if she woke up in the morning and found the whole thing a dream? What if she'd accidentally taken too many anxiety pills and this was some sort of weird hallucination?

She wanted to remember what they looked like.

As she studied them now she appreciated the differences in the images. The rooms had a slight feminine feel to them that were oddly gentle against the darkness. They were clean and bright, but sadly lacking any personality. The rugs were bright, their colors cheerful, and care had been taken in choosing them since they matched but there weren't any knickknacks or flowers in vases. Just rooms, simple and tidy.

Sitting back, she smiled to herself as she put her paintbrushes away. It was dawn. She had been given a gift. After all these years, she'd finally been given something useful. She'd used her imagination and talent to try to help clients see the past. Now, for once, *she'd* been able to see it herself. It would probably never happen again, and it wasn't quite like going back in time, but it was a jolt she'd certainly never forget.

So, the house was a little creepy and apparently bad enough to keep vandals out, but that didn't really concern her. She wasn't there to hurt it; she was there to make it come alive. She might not have believed in much when it came to the afterlife or religion, but she *did* believe in positive thinking. If she ignored the bad and focused on the good, then surely the house would work with her, right? Whatever was there had been dead and gone for a long, long time. And the past couldn't hurt her. At least, not *this* past. This wasn't her past, after all. This was someone else's past.

Then, why, suddenly, did she feel like crying?

. . .

She hadn't planned on sleeping past noon, but since she'd seen the sun come up, Taryn really didn't see a way around it. She needed more than just a few hours' worth of sleep if she was going to be able to function at all. Still, as she pulled herself into the small diner on the outskirts of town she felt jetlagged and disoriented. The young waitress looked at her sympathetically as she handed her a menu. "Can I get you something to drink?"

"Something with a lot of caffeine," she muttered. She'd start doing that tomorrow.

"I hear that," she laughed. She was tall and willowy and wore braces. Taryn estimated her to be anywhere from sixteen to twenty-five, but the braces threw her off. "I'm having one of those days myself."

"You recommend anything?"

She shrugged. "We make everything, so it's all okay. Well, except for anything with fruit. That usually comes in a can unless it's summer, like now. I like the pancakes myself."

Handing her back the menu, Taryn nodded. "I'll take those then. And some sausage. And hey, are you from around here?"

"All my life, why?"

Taking a moment, Taryn described the house she was in town for. "Let me go put your order in and I'll be right back."

The restaurant was empty and she busied herself going through the pictures on her digital camera, still marveling at the images that shouldn't be there, until the waitress came back. Sliding into the seat across from her, she leaned into Taryn and started chatting. "You don't mind if I smoke, do you?"

"I didn't know anywhere still let you do that."

"Well, they don't," she said. "But nobody around here says anything or cares."

Taryn waited patiently while her waitress sat back and blew a few puffs, the white rings drifting off into the aisle and floating toward the empty counter. The sounds of dishes and silverware rattling back in the kitchen were the only noises in the otherwise quiet room. She must have missed the lunch crowd.

"I know the house, of course. Everyone does. It's kind of the town haunted house, if you know what I mean. Some people called it 'the Devil's house' growing up or just 'the stone gate to hell' because the gate out front is made of stone. Well, you know. We used to dare each other to go in there as kids. As teenagers, really. I'm Tammy, by the way."

"Taryn."

"Nice to meet you," she smiled, revealing her braces again. "Why you asking about the old place? You thinking of poking around in it?"

"Well, actually, I'm working there for a while," Taryn explained. "I've already poked." She took a few minutes and explained what she was doing and then laughed when Tammy shuddered.

"Better you than me, girlfriend, better you than me." When Tammy smiled, her face lit up and she possessed the kind of easygoing all-American beauty that Taryn envied. Even in her waitress uniform and braces, she managed to be pretty and perky. In contrast, Taryn still felt tired and haggard and her wrinkled khaki capris and buttoned-down western shirt (a size too big) made her feel dowdy.

"You ever go in there?" she asked, sensing a story waiting to be told.

"Once," Tammy answered conspiratorially. "But never any further than the kitchen. I was with my boyfriend at the time. We were sophomores. He'd just gotten his license, you know? Second day. It was the Friday after Thanksgiving and it was kind of cold like. There was a group of us and everyone else was poking around the property. Smoking, walking around. Just being kids, really. We decided to go *in* the house. Nobody else would. Lots of stories about that place, you know? Everyone daring everyone else to go in, but not too many people really did it. Anyway, we were going to be all brave and do it. So we walked up to the door, my boyfriend being all macho, and he pushed it in. We stepped inside and he pulled out the flashlight. He goes first. It is **dead** quiet. Steps in, looks around. Says it's okay. I go in. He's all the way in the other room by the time I go inside. I'm halfway through the kitchen when he starts running back through the house and he's out the door. I have no idea why so I just stand there, kind of frozen like. Then I saw it. Well, first I heard it." Tammy shivered at the memory and snuffed out her cigarette into a saucer.

"What was it?" Without realizing it, Taryn leaned forward.

"A cry. It was the longest, saddest cry I'd ever heard in my life," Tammy whispered. "It came from upstairs. A woman. Well, a girl, really. Maybe my age. Like it was just breaking your heart. It shook the whole house. I felt it all the way down to my toes. I knew that cry. I've cried like that myself when my own heart was breaking. You know when you've had a breakup or felt like nobody loved you and your world was ending?" Tammy stopped talking and waited for Taryn to concede.

Not knowing quite how to answer, Taryn glanced down at the table and fiddled with her straw wrapper. "I know what you're talking about. Hey, I was a teenager once, right?" She said the last part hurriedly, hoping Tammy would continue. She did.

"I heard that and wanted to cry along with her. I couldn't move. But then I *did* move because right after that, this figure appeared in the kitchen door. It was solid black and it wanted me. Don't ask me how I knew—I just did. It was coming for me. It felt evil. You know what I mean? I turned and ran out of that house as fast as I could but I could feel it watching me all the way to the car. I will never forget it."

Tammy shivered again and rolled her eyes. "Sometimes, in my sleep, I still hear that cry. You know, the shadow, the evil thing? It bothered me, it scared me. But it was that cry, it was that sound that still bothers me. I'll never forget it as long as I live. I still don't know what my boyfriend saw. He won't talk about it."

She gazed absently out the window at the passing cars and Taryn studied her. She had no reason to doubt her story, especially since it rang familiar. In fact, Taryn figured most people believed in the stories they told you, and there was a little grain of truth in everything.

The two women sat in companionable silence for a few moments, each one last in their own thoughts. A bell at the window rang and Tammy jumped up and brought Taryn's pancakes to her. "There are others in town that might be able to tell you their own stories. There have been stories about that place for years, ever since my mom was a little girl."

"Did anything happen there? I mean, is there a story? Did anyone die?"

"Not that I know of," Tammy replied. "I mean, not tragically or anything. Just old age and stuff like that. But I can talk to my grandma. She knows most of that stuff. Here, I'll give you my email." Hurriedly, Tammy jotted her information down on a slip of paper and then went back into the kitchen again.

. . .

Obviously, it wasn't the first time Taryn had heard a ghost story about the place she was painting. All old houses were meant to be haunted. It was almost an insult if they weren't. She had found that if there weren't any real tales to be told about the place, people were generally happy enough to make them up.

Tammy had seemed perfectly reliable and honest. But there were many reasons why a person might see or hear something in an old house. Taryn explained similar stories away for years. She had to. If she didn't, she might never step foot inside some of the places she worked in.

But she couldn't deny that Tammy's story had given her chills, chills like the ones she herself had felt inside the house. There was something going on inside and apparently more than one person had picked up on it. She needed to remember that. This house was different. She couldn't shrug these stories off like she had the others. Not after what she saw on her camera.

Once, on a job site in Georgia, she'd been painting a picture of an old plantation home. Most of it was no longer erect, but the local historical society received a grant to restore it. They had brought in Taryn, along with an architect, to create images of it.

Taryn didn't care for working with other people, but the architect was a young man her own age, just out of college, and he was friendly. He, too, preferred working on his own, so their paths didn't cross much and, when they did, it wasn't unpleasant. They'd both shared a love of history and the antebellum style of the home. Both were equally glad it was being restored.

Two weeks into the job, Taryn arrived onsite and found him standing outside, staring at the crumbling porch. He had a look on his face that was a cross between bemusement and horror. She touched his shoulder and he jumped into the air in shock.

"I'm sorry," he apologized. "I must have been thinking."

"Is everything okay?" she asked, feeling foolish because everything was obviously not okay.

He led her to a weeping willow tree and both sat down under it, the house in plain view in front of them. It was a beautiful structure with four large columns (signs of wealth) and a porch that had, at one time, stretched the length of the front. Even in its decay, she saw beauty in it and what it could be again one day.

"I crawled in through one of the back windows this morning," he said softly. "I know it's not safe, but well, you know…"

She nodded. Of course, she did it all the time. She had also done it here to this house, too.

"It was so quiet and peaceful. I walked around to the front of the house, real careful with my footing, and stayed where I knew the foundation was solid. There's a mantel in there that just blew my mind. Can't believe how perfect it is, considering that half the house is falling in."

Taryn let him talk without interruption, even though he kept taking long breaks in his speech.

"I wasn't inside for more than ten minutes, when I heard this sound. I wasn't sure what it was at first. It sounded like music. I thought maybe you were here and had your car radio on. I don't know. But something didn't feel right about it. Then, I realized it was coming from inside the house. And it wasn't a radio at all, but a piano."

The house was devoid of furnishings. There was no piano anywhere near it. They were at least five miles from the nearest inhabited house.

"Are you sure?" Taryn asked tentatively, but she knew he was certain of what he heard.

He nodded. "It went on for a few minutes and I just stood there and listened. It was maybe the most beautiful piano music I've ever heard. It felt as close as if I could just walk into the parlor and see someone sitting there, playing. And then it stopped. I thought it was over, but that's when the laughing started. A high, feminine laugh. A woman's for sure. It echoed through the rooms, like the sound was being soaked into the walls."

"What did you do?"

"I got out," he shrugged. "I couldn't do it."

Taryn knew he was confident in what he had heard. She knew he wasn't making the story up. She had spent many hours there in the house by herself and had felt like someone was watching her, listening to her talk to herself sometimes. But she'd never seen anything. She'd never heard anything. Sitting there under the tree with him, she almost felt disappointment.

. . .

She spent a productive day at the house, her experiences from her previous visits not repeated. She even tried walking around, taking more pictures, but they came out like any other picture she'd ever taken. *Maybe it's just my imagination*, she thought to herself. She probably *did* need more sleep.

The house felt quiet, at peace. In fact, the day was amazingly calm and still. It was a day straight out of a summer calendar: the birds were chirping, the butterflies flew about, the bees buzzed, and the clouds were fat and white against the bright blue sky. With her sandals kicked off and the grass curled up between her toes, Taryn was at a rare ease with herself. She listened to Bruce Robison and Tift Merritt while she worked, alternating their CDs and singing along when the spirit moved her.

The sketching went amazingly fast and within the first day she had most of the house outlined to her satisfaction. Taryn enjoyed standing outside and working in this park-like setting. She appreciated the fact that even though there were adjoining farms on either side of her (well, one was being developed as she worked) she rarely heard any kind of passing vehicle.

As she sketched, she thought about the house's former tenants. What had they been like? Had they thrown parties, celebrated a lot, worked hard? And what about the poor girl who had died? Taryn hoped she hadn't suffered much. The scent of decay and death were still overpowering at times, but she was starting to think that perhaps the house was picking up on some of the tragedies it had seen over the years: first Robert's wife and then his daughter.

Taryn also appreciated the fact that the Stokes County Historical Society had contracted her at all. She could use the money especially since she wasn't completely sure her car was going to hold up much longer. And the hotel wasn't bad either; at least, not as far as hotels went. The swimming pool was kind of nice and the free breakfast was more than just cereal and bananas. And then, of course, there was the bonus of it having indoor corridors—*always* a sign she was staying in a swanky place.

But she wasn't sleeping well, and she was tired. Taryn's dreams had bothered her over the past few nights; however, ever since she arrived in Vidalia (and what about that town name?). The previous night (morning) she dreamed she was falling into something dark and then awakened to the sound of crying. She was sure it had been someone else's cries at first, but since the dream had shaken her so much, she wasn't positive it hadn't been her own tears that woke her up.

And then there was the dream of being suffocated and unable to move. That was the worst one. It caused her to thrash about in her bed, as though held by ropes. She'd woken up struggling with her pillows and had slept with the TV on ever since. It might mean she was hearing used car commercials all night, but at least it offered her light and noise.

. . .

At the end of the day, after loading everything into the car, Taryn slipped her sandals back on and went for a walk around the property. With the boards off the door and windows, the house appeared more inviting. The stones were polished and reflected the late afternoon sunlight; the wide front porch easy to envision a swing and rocking chair on and full of guests enjoying the evening after a hard day's work. Taryn's appreciated talent might have been in showing the world what the past looked like, but her real talent was in imagining what the past held. Sometimes, it wasn't always welcomed. Sometimes it even hurt.

Staring at the contrast between the older part of the house and addition and holding her camera in her hands, Taryn felt the weight of the day on her shoulders. "Off to a good start," she whispered. "Going well." The house seemed to shimmer in the light, as if agreeing with her. A ripple of cool air sent chill bumps along her legs and up her arms. She continued walking but crossed her arms over her chest.

Behind the house, the air was lighter and it was a little easier to breathe. It was also less magical somehow. She turned on her camera again and looked at the pictures she had taken that day. They were all normal images. But the ones before them, those, well, they were the special ones. *Yep*, she thought, *still there*. She hadn't dreamed them. *I'm not going crazy.*

It was during this time of the day that she should be winding down and feeling good about what she had done, but it was usually by now when she felt the loneliest. She wasn't due to talk to Matt tonight, although she knew she could call him and probably should, especially after what happened. The sinking feeling in the pit of her stomach that had plagued her for months and months was getting better there for a while, but she imagined she would always suffer setbacks.

When the last rays of light had fallen behind the barn, she made her way back to her car and got in. She didn't know why people were so afraid of the house; it just seemed sad to her.

Available on Rebecca's Website at www.rebeccaphoward.net

A BROOM WITH A VIEW
Excerpt

She's your average witch next door.
He's a Christmas tree farmer with three sisters named after horses.
It's a town so small it doesn't even have a Walmart.
None of them will ever be the same again...

Chapter One

LIZA JANE HIGGINBOTHAM was a witch.

Mind you, not the kind of witch that conversed with black cats or could make herself look like a supermodel with a wave of her hand (although that skill would've been useful on several occasions) but a witch, nonetheless.

When she was twelve she'd watched a movie about a girl who came into her witchy powers on her sixteenth birthday. "Teen Witch," it was called.

She wasn't *that* kind of witch either.

Liza Jane had been born a witch, known it most of her life, and considered it as normal as her hair color.

(Okay, maybe not *quite* as normal as her hair color. Thanks to Clairol and some plastic gloves, she'd been dying her hair for so long she had no idea what her natural color was.)

Nope, she thought as she gave the last box on the U-Haul a good, solid kick with her tennis shoe and sent it flying down the icy ramp, *she was just a regular witch with few useful and exciting skills.*

Sure, she could get rid of negative energy around a place, was a pretty good healer, and could see into the future with a little bit of help from some of her tools—but she couldn't make herself invisible or turn people into frogs.

Had she been a *TV* kind of witch, she'd have just wrinkled her nose a few times and in an orderly fashion sent those boxes flying into the house, where they then would've graciously unpacked themselves. Then she would've spent the rest of the afternoon lounging on a perfectly made bed (*not* made by her, of course), watching Rom-Coms, and feeding herself strawberries.

And later she would've turned Jennifer Miller into a cockroach. Just for the fun of it.

But she could *not* send all the boxes into the house like that, she couldn't afford to get cable, and there were no strawberries available in Kudzu Valley in December.

Shivering even inside her thermal coat, Liza Jane rubbed her chapped hands together and hopped down from the back of the truck. She blew out a puff of air, her breath making a large round cloud before floating away and watched as the box slid off the ramp and landed with a thud at the bottom. One side was completely caved in. She hoped there wasn't anything breakable in it. She hadn't taken the time to mark any of them. It was going to be complete chaos for a while.

Divorce was making her more unorganized than usual.

And she was still a little miffed that she'd missed Thanksgiving back north. But she'd had to get out of there as quickly as possible. She'd had to, even if it meant eating chicken nuggets and fries instead of turkey.

"What the *hell* was I thinking?" she muttered to herself as she turned and looked at her new house.

Well, technically, her *old* house. She had lived there, once upon a time. She'd been six then and now she was in her thirties, so it had been...

Well, she didn't need to think about how many years ago that was. She was already depressed enough as it was.

Her grandparents' white farm house rose before her in the dreary winter sky, proud and neglected. White paint had chipped off and now sprinkled the dead, brown grass like dirty snow, leaving behind naked patches of worn wood. An upstairs window was boarded up, the glass missing. A black garbage bag covered another. A window unit in the second-floor master bedroom had leaked and dripped over the years, leaving a stream of discolored water running down the side of the house. She was almost certain the front porch was leaning, too.

Liza Jane cocked her head to one side and studied it. *Yep*, she thought, *it was definitely crooked.*

"At least it has electricity and running water," she stated cheerfully.

Nothing answered her back. She was surrounded by more than fifty acres of mountainside and pastureland. Her grandparents' farm. Her *family* farm. Her heritage.

Damn, it was dismal.

She knew it would look better in the summertime, when the trees were bursting and full of leaves and color, the fields were lush with wildflowers and thick grass, and the sky a brilliant blue.

But for now everything was dead. Dead and gray. Even the tree branches were gray. How was that *possible*?

Her divorce was almost final. She just needed to sign the papers. Her high school sweetheart had left her for the woman at Starbucks who made him his latte every morning. (Well, actually he was marrying the trombone player in the pop opera group he managed. He'd just initially left her for the Starbucks chick. There had, apparently, been many women. Many, *many* women.)

Back in Boston she'd lost her interesting and well-paying job as the administrative assistant to the director at the nonprofit organization she'd been with for two years. She'd been unceremoniously fired when everyone on her floor, including some donors, overheard her yelling obscenities over the phone to her husband's lawyer.

She'd let the happy new couple have her house in Wakefield. She'd loved that house, had enjoyed everything about it. But once she'd discovered that Latte-Girl had gotten busy on her kitchen table and Trombone Chick had blown more than her mouthpiece on Liza Jane's $2,000 leather sofa, the bloom kind of fell off the rose.

"You're being very immature about this," her husband, Mode, had told her when she'd handed him her house key.

In her mind, Liza had stuck her tongue out at him and snarked, *I thought you thought people overused the word "very."* Instead, she'd kept her face impassive.

"You own this house outright," he'd continued, growing increasingly agitated by her lack of fight. "You don't have a job. You won't be able to support yourself. Your money will run out soon. You've *never* been good at money management, Liza. It makes no sense for you to leave the house. Jennifer and I will be fine someplace else. We won't have any problems settling in." He'd paused at that moment and leaned in closer to her. Then, with their faces only inches apart, he'd put his hand on her arm. "It's *you* I'm worried about."

His self-righteousness had been the last straw. She'd told him where he could stick her house key.

Now, since she'd signed over the house to him and he'd given her half its appraised worth, she was moving back into the only other thing she owned besides her ratty car–her grandparents' dilapidated farm house in Kudzu Valley, Kentucky.

Liza Jane was depressed.

"Promise me you won't kill yourself," her mother, Mabel, had shrilled over the phone on Liza's drive down. "Nobody would even know forever, you being out there by yourself like that!"

"Please consider medication or a therapist," Mode had cajoled her with fake worry and sincerity.

"Don't do anything stupid down there," her younger sister, Bryar Rose, had warned her. "Like join Scientology or get bangs."

"Well, maybe just a *little* something," she muttered, flipping her hair back from her face, her teeth chattering in the gusty wind.

For a moment, the air around her stilled. The time-honored words she chanted ascended from her like a soft breeze, comforting her with their familiarity and cadence. They gently lifted the ends of her hair and swept across her face like motherly hands, their warmth nearly bringing tears to her eyes. Her heart raced and for just a second she felt a surge of adrenalin, like she could take on the world if she wanted.

And then it stopped.

Grinning with satisfaction, Liza opened her eyes and studied the farm house again. The porch was perfectly straight, not a board out of place.

"Yeah, well, I deserved it," she snapped to the crows that flew overhead.

Then, feeling a little drained and hung over from what she'd just done, Liza Jane proudly marched up her new steps and into her new life.

. . .

When Liza Jane had last been in Kudzu Valley it had boasted a Taco Bell, Burger King, and McDonalds. There was talk back then of putting in a Walmart on the new by-pass that circled around the mountain and circumvented the small downtown area that consisted of two cross streets and one red light.

That Walmart never materialized; the by-pass was a lonesome stretch of road that passed through what used to be farm land and a drive-in. Five families had lost land to it all in the name of progress. It did, however, get travelers to the next county over three minutes faster. This was important since Morel County was dry, making it impossible to (legally) buy any kind of alcohol.

Liza's grandfather, Paine, had died ten years earlier. Her grandmother, Nana Bud, had passed away two years ago. The old farm house had been empty ever since, although it had been winterized and a neighbor had watched over it and taken care of any repairs it needed.

Liza had gone down and taken a look at things back in the summer, before her big move, so she kind of knew what she was getting herself into. Still, there weren't many conveniences. For one thing, it was completely devoid of food, unless you wanted to count the bag of birdseed that someone (her grandfather probably) had left out on the back porch in the 1980s and the small piece of moldy cheese that had led a mouse to his last fatal adventure.

Liza Jane needed supplies.

Other than the tiny food marts attached to some of the gas stations, there was only one grocery store in the entire county. It was a discount chain that sold fatty beef, bait, generic canned food, and bulk bags of cheap cereal.

She could roll with that. At least it was cheap. And right now she needed cheap. She was not only moving to Kudzu Valley, she was opening her own business. The money her grandmother had left her two years ago and the divorce settlement would not last forever.

She'd declined alimony.

As Liza slowly pushed her cart down the unfamiliar aisles and loaded up with boxes of Rice Crisps and Frosty Tiny Wheats, Liza became acutely aware of someone's eyes drilling holes into her.

Her senses stayed at a heightened state of awareness these days; when she'd let them slide in the past her husband had gone on a one-man tour of the local single ladies and she wasn't going to make *that* mistake again. However, she did try to turn her senses down when she was out in public so that she didn't pick up on every Dick, Jane, and Bubba's feelings and thoughts but even a Normal would've felt the sharp eyes stabbing into their back.

"Liza Jane Merriweather!" The loud, reedy shrill came from less than ten feet behind her and had Liza startled, despite her mindfulness.

When she turned, Liza was face to face with a tiny, elderly woman carrying a yellow shopping basket overflowing with at least two dozen packages of frozen spinach. Unlike many of the other shoppers, who looked like they'd stumbled out of bed without getting dressed or brushing their hair or teeth, the little woman before her wore a blue-tailored suit and was in full makeup.

Her lavender eyeshadow framed small, beady eyes behind thick bifocals and her clunky heels sounded like shotgun blasts as she marched over to where Liza Jane patiently waited. Her hair, permed and sprayed within an inch of its life, was a brilliant purple.

Liza closed her eyes for a moment and reached forward, focusing on the woman's mind. She frantically attempted to extract a name or memory, since it was obvious she was meant to know the person whose arms were now outstretched and gearing up for a hug.

The only word she could come up with was "Pebbles."

"Just look at *you!*" the woman crooned, squeezing Liza Jane in a bony, yet tight, embrace. The combination of Marlboro Lights, Aqua Net, and Elizabeth Taylor's White Diamonds was almost overpowering. "You're so grown up now!"

Liza plastered what she hoped was a respectful smile across her face and gently untangled herself. She was afraid to squeeze back too hard; despite the woman's grip her shoulders and arms felt brittle. God forbid she break somebody on her first day out in town.

"Yes," she replied courteously. "I've grown up a little."

"Liza Jane Merriweather," the woman murmured again, shaking her head in apparent disbelief. Her hair didn't move an inch. Liza had to restrain herself from reaching out and touching it. "I just *can't* believe it."

"Well, actually it's Higginbotham now," Liza helpfully corrected her. "I got married."

"Oh?" At the mention of a husband the woman's eyes sparkled. "Is he here with you?" She began looking around, as though Liza might have hidden him under a gallon of milk in her shopping cart.

"Err..." Liza felt her face turning red. "He's um, back in Boston. We're still, uh, getting some things together. For the move down here."

There was no need to go into the messy details of her impending divorce right there in the grocery store aisle. People were already stopping, pretending to be keenly interested in the nutritional values on the backs of discount cereal boxes while they listened to the two women chat.

"Oh, well, that's okay. I bet you don't remember my name. Do you remember my name," she demanded.

Liza, taken off guard, found herself flustered as she regarded the impatient woman. She reached out again but came back with nothing. If she'd known her in the past, it was as a child and she'd made little to no impression on Liza.

"Well, I er, I *think* so..." Liza murmured, embarrassed. *Give me a break, lady, it's been almost thirty years*, she thought to herself at the same time.

"It's *Penny*! Penny Libbels!" she cried, slapping Liza Jane on the arm with unexpected strength. "I was your granny's best friend, may she rest in peace."

"Oh, *Pebbles*," Liza Jane nodded now. "Okay, that makes more sense."

"You never *could* say my name right." Penny stared at her wide-eyed and Liza wondered if she was waiting for her to try to say it *now*.

"Um, well, I was young I guess," Liza faltered.

Liza had never been particularly good at small talk. Or grocery stores.

"I hear that you're opening one of those New Agey herbal shops here," Penny pressed, squinting her purple eyes under the harsh fluorescent lights. "You aren't gonna be selling those *drugs* are you? That *meth*?"

At least three more people stopped what they were doing and turned to look back at them, not even trying to hide their curiosity. Liza randomly grabbed at a can of pineapples behind her and clutched it tightly, its metal hard and reassuring under her fingertips. She was about to dig a hole into her hands from the wringing and had already popped an acrylic.

"Well, um, no," she sputtered. "Nothing illegal. It's a holistic clinic, a day spa really, with herbal remedies and massages and– "

"Not one of those places with *hookers*," Penny lowered her voice to a stage whisper, her eyes darting around as she pursed her lips.

"Oh no! Just teas and lotions and regular old massages. Nothing bad," Liza promised.

Oh, dear Lord, make me disappear, she prayed silently.

Liza thought she might pass out. One woman passing by actually grabbed her young son by the arm and pushed him ahead of her, as though Liza was already a lady of the night, hawking her body and illegal drugs in the fruit and cereal aisle.

"Hmmm," Penny pursed her lips again so tightly they were almost white. "Well, you *might* do okay here. We're not Hollywood, though. I don't know how many people need those New Agey things. We got a," her voice dropped back down to a stage whisper, "*chiropractor* last year."

Liza nodded her head, pretending to understand the implication.

"He's just *now* starting to catch on," Penny continued. "The ladies here are good Christian women and they don't like being touched in certain places by men who aren't their husbands. But I suppose since you're a woman, it will be just fine."

Penny did not look hopeful.

It was now all Liza Jane could do to keep a straight face. The can of pineapples began to shake in her unsteady hands as she forced her body to control itself. She mentally gathered her thoughts together and forced her breathing to slow down and ease up. Then she ran a quick, but effective, little charm through her mind that sent a wave of coolness through her body, relaxing her muscles and nerves. It wasn't much, but it would hold until she reached the check-out counter.

"Well, I certainly hope people will give me a chance," Liza replied diplomatically once she'd collected herself together.

"Well, at least you don't *have* to work since your husband has a good job. Rosebud was always bragging about his work with the music group. I'm sure your little business will get along just fine and dandy. It's nice for a lady to have a hobby these days," Penny crooned, patting Liza Jane on the arm. "I'd better skedaddle now. I'm making a pot roast for dinner after church tomorrow. Have you found a church yet?"

"I, er..."

"Never mind. You're coming to mine! Elk Creek Primitive. We don't allow none of that singing or music nonsense that the Baptists and Methodists seem to carry on about, but you'll *love* our services. They run all morning and our preacher truly gets the spirit deep inside him. I will see you at ten!"

Before Liza could answer, Penny was scurrying off through the considerable number of onlookers, her purple hair a helmet raging her into battle towards the produce.

Since it was a dry county and beer was unavailable, Liza turned and headed back to the candy aisle.

She was going to need a lot more chocolate than she'd initially planned for.

. . .

Despite the old house's "quirks" (she was going to call them "quirks" because, at the moment, that sounded less intimidating than "problems") she loved it. It was spacious and full of charm and character.

More importantly, it smelled and *felt* like her grandparents, and she missed them something fierce. She hadn't visited them nearly as much as she'd wanted to as a child, and hardly at all as an adult. Still, they had regularly gone north and visited Liza, her mother, and her sister on the major holidays and during Paine's vacations.

Liza had looked forward to their visits more than she'd looked forward to the holidays themselves.

Liza didn't think there was a finer woman in the world than her Nana Bud had been, and most everyone who'd known Rosebud in her lifetime would have probably agreed.

Liza's heart had broken when Rosebud passed away.

Her death was especially difficult for Liza since she'd been in Spain with her husband at the time and, due to the standard form of miscommunication exhibited by her mother and Bryar Rose, she hadn't found out about it until her grandmother was already dead and in the ground.

Liza, filled with grief she didn't know she was capable of feeling (she didn't remember her father *or* his death) she'd lashed out at everyone from her husband to the poor plumber who'd just come to the house to unclog the guest toilet. In fact, her relationship with her sister Bryar was still strained and had only started to improve when talk of her divorce from Mode began.

Nothing brought sisters, or women in general, together more than a shared enemy, and Bryar always *had* enjoyed being in the middle of drama.

Liza regretted not attending the funeral; she was even more ashamed that she hadn't seen her grandmother in more than a year when she died. She'd always assumed there would be more time.

She guessed everyone thought that.

Liza Jane thought the guilt of not being there for someone who loved you and having nobody to blame but yourself had to be one of the most dreadful feelings in the world. It was for her, anyway. Rather than being at her grandmother's side, she'd been following her husband around like a puppy on the beaches of Marbella during breaks while he gawked at the topless women and their rosy nipples.

She'd been there when her grandfather Paine had passed away peacefully at the Hospice Center. She'd even been holding his hand when it happened. But that was different.

She'd loved her grandfather but hadn't known him well. He'd always been a quiet, gentle soul who didn't offer much of himself to anyone but his wife. And he'd lived a good, long life. When he'd passed on, Liza had been sad but it had felt *right*. He'd suffered for so long; his death was as much as a relief as it was a release.

As soon as they're returned from England, the last leg of the tour, Liza had locked herself in the guest room. It was the only place in the house Mode said he felt comfortable with her keeping her "supplies" as he called them. (He'd always claimed he was fine with her being a witch and had even considered it a fun little novelty at first, but now Liza was convinced that he'd been partly afraid of her. And rightly so. He *should* have been afraid. Very afraid.)

She'd stayed in that room for two days, holding her own vigil for Nana Bud. On her altar, she'd lit candles and placed Rosebud's picture and some of the cards she'd sent Liza over the years. She'd chanted, she'd meditated, and she'd offered thanks for having someone like her in her life. She'd called to the elements and sought peace within herself.

Mostly, she grieved.

Mode had left her alone. When she'd emerged at the end of the second day, hungry and exhausted, he'd glanced up from a Science Fiction book he was reading and asked her what she wanted for supper, like she'd just returned home from the movies.

"Jerkwad," Liza muttered now as she remembered the moment in total clarity.

Not all witches were made alike. While they could do similar things and for similar reasons, they were all individuals and had their own unique traits. Unfortunately, sometimes for Liza, one of her strongest traits was that she could remember things that happened ten years ago in total, accurate detail as though they'd occurred just moments earlier. She wished that gift had kicked in while her father was still alive but, like some of the other things she'd learned about herself, witchery and the skills it entailed seemed to be an ongoing process.

But as for Mode..." *Jerkwad*" was one of the nicest things she'd called him. When *his* grandmother had died, she'd been there for him. She'd even arranged the funeral, since both of Mode's parents were dead.

And she'd taken care of all the guests who had filed in and out of the house after the internment. He, on the other hand, never brought up *her* grandmother again. Didn't even offer to send flowers to the cemetery.

Asshat.

Now, as she paced alone through the rooms of the old farm house and touched its walls, feeling the same places her grandparents had also touched, she could feel a part of them near her. It was both peaceful and comforting, even when thoughts of Mode threatened to tear her up inside. (Asshat or Jerkwad aside, they *had* been married for a long time and she *was* grieving a part of him–the part she wanted him to be anyway.)

The overstuffed chairs covered in rainbow-colored afghans held imprints from their bottoms. The stale scent of cigarette smoke (even after being diagnosed with lung cancer her Papaw Paine hadn't given up his Marlboros) that still lingered in the air even after eight years, lace doilies on every flat surface, hundreds of ceramic teapots and ladybug statues, and homemade rag rugs scattered throughout the house were constant reminders of the two people who'd meant the world to her.

Liza vaguely remembered living there in the house with her mother and sister after her father died but those memories felt more like dreams. Still, while they might not have been strong, something about the house *felt* like home anyway. When she'd returned to Kudzu Valley to take stock of the situation after her separation from Mode, she'd known instantly that the idea she was flirting with in her mind was the right one.

As soon as she'd turned off the main road and entered the downtown proper, a calmness had settled over her. The mountains were lush with leaves then, their colors almost unnatural. She'd rolled down her windows and deeply inhaled the town right there on Main Street.

The air itself tasted of freedom.

And when the old farm house had come into view, despite the headache she was getting from the various washouts in the gravel, she'd *felt* her name being called, not heard.

Liza had no experience when it came to living in the country, or even living in a small town—at least no recent experience.

"You lived at home for college for Chrissakes!" her mother had scolded her. "You've never even been responsible for a house by yourself!"

Which was true, unless you wanted to consider the fact that Mode only did what he thought he *had* to.

"You've never lived more than a ten-minute walk to a store," her sister had pointed out, which was *also* true, although to Bryar "the Boondocks" meant someplace that couldn't get Chinese delivered to you thirty minutes or less.

At least in her adult life, Liza had *never* lived in isolation, never lived without neighbors within a stone's throw distance, never lived without an active nightlife and restaurant scene just minutes away (now, if she wanted to go to a nightclub, she'd have to drive for more than an hour and a half) and had never been responsible for only herself.

Hell, she'd only even lived by herself just recently. After moving out she'd ended up renting a dinky little apartment in Beverly that cost a fortune but had a closet the size of a shoebox and a view of a couple who were either newlyweds or just really, really amorous.

Still, standing there in the yard, *her* yard now, and feeling the ground beneath her feet—the same ground generations of her relatives had stood on as well, she knew she was home.

She knew it as a witch; she knew it as a woman.

"You can *have* it," Bryar Rose had sworn as soon as Liza asked her permission to move into it. "What the hell am I going to do with it?"

Her mother had echoed the sentiment.

She didn't remember the shotgun house on Ann Street where she'd lived with her real father or the trips to the local park she'd apparently taken with him when he was alive (though she'd seen the pictures). Her only memories of Kudzu Valley had come from her brief and infrequent visits growing up. In her college sociology class, however, she'd read about how people from Appalachia could get the mountains in their blood and never really shake them. No matter where they went, the mountains stayed with them, softly beckoning them to return home.

Liza figured she was one of those people. All those years of living in the city, she'd teared up every time she'd watched "Matewan" or "Coal Miner's Daughter" or even "Next of Kin" and "Justified." Movies set in eastern Kentucky or nearby had pulled at her, even the bad ones, and she'd watched the credits feeling a yearning, like she was missing something she'd never even had.

. . .

The farm house had four bedrooms and two had actual bedroom furniture. Another was what looked like her grandmother had used for a junk room. It was a mess but, more importantly, if she was going to get that board off the window and replace the glass she'd have to straighten it up. As it was, there was no direct path to get to the other side of the room.

There wasn't a *path* at all.

The room was full of boxes of patterns dating back to the 1970s, scraps of random material, Christmas tree lights, bags of unopened junk mail, and boxes of 3-ply toilet paper. Seriously, there was more toilet paper than two people could ever use. And her grandfather had been gone for a long time.

"Aw Nana Bud," Liza chuckled. "You really got the use out of your Sam's Club membership, didn't you?"

Well, at least she wouldn't have to stock up on that necessity any time soon. Nana Bud had always believed in being prepared; you could never have too much toilet paper or chicken broth.

She bought both every time she left the house, even if it was to just make a run to the post office.

With Luke Bryan blaring on the portable CD player she'd found in the room she was using as her own bedroom, Liza sashayed around, singing along and bobbing her head in time with the music while she sorted and organized.

She'd listened to country music stations on the whole ride down. It might have sounded stupid to others, but one of the things that excited her about living in Kudzu Valley was the thought of being a part of those things the songs talked about: a sense of community, bonfires with neighbors, and adventurous drives down backroads that turned to dirt...

After what she'd been through with Mode and his menagerie of extracurricular activities, she couldn't wait to dive into the bucolic life those singers crooned about and live a more peaceful existence.

Goodbye to pop opera bands, naked boobs on the beach, and 2:00 am Chinese. Hello to four wheeling (whatever that *really* was), horseback riding (she could learn), and gardening (she *did* have a green thumb).

When Luke got into his song about the woman dancing in his truck, Liza, who was in the middle of bending over to pick up an old tennis racket, paused mid-air.

Did she need a truck?

Oh, she thought with glee. *Maybe I **do** need a truck.*

The idea thrilled her to the bone—the thought of cruising through town sitting high above the road, being able to haul...stuff.

But she changed her mind as quickly as the idea came to her. She *had* a car and Christabel had been good to her. More than that, when she made the payment on her next week, she'd own her free and clear.

And it only took six years.

"Okay, okay," she grumbled aloud, just in case Christabel had been able to hear her thoughts and desires from her position in the driveway. There were times when Liza was certain her car had a sixth sense, but she hadn't been able to prove it yet. "No truck for me. I have a good car."

Sighing with regret, Liza leaned back over to reach for the tennis racket again and then popped back up.

"Hey," she cried, her eyes bright with excitement. "Do I need a *gun*?!"

A heavy box of books fell off the top of a shelf just then and came within a hair of crashing down on her toes. Liza had reacted quickly enough that she was able to stop it mid-air and gently move it a few feet to the left before letting it continue its drop.

"Yeah, yeah, yeah," she muttered again. "I hear you. Grandpa. Or Nana. Or whichever one of my dead relatives you might be. I won't get a gun. I don't even know how to use one."

Before returning to work Liza did stop and listen to the room for a few minutes, however. If there *had* been another energy there moments ago, it was gone now.

If either one of her grandparents had been watching over her, and in the very room with her, they were no longer there.

Liza was sorry about that.

Chapter Two

PROSTITUTE RUMORS aside, Liza Jane really felt like her life was going to fall into place in Kudzu Valley.

Her new business, The Healing Hands, was on the corner of Main Street and Broadway. At one time Kudzu Valley had been a thriving railroad town, a town built to house the workers of the tracks that ran right through the middle of downtown. The houses and businesses were all laid out in a perfect grid, a perfectly planned community.

At one time the town boasted not one but *two* cinemas, a handful of restaurants, two department stores, and several dozen locally-owned businesses.

There had even been a drive-in and Liza could almost remember going to it as a child, sitting on the hood of the car with nachos and popcorn between her and a man who was now blurry in her mind.

However, things had changed. More of the storefronts were empty than used now, their dusty windows overlooking a street that saw little traffic. Liza expected to see a tumbleweed blow by at any moment.

A crazy part of her considered running out in the middle of the road and laying down under the one and only red light, just to see how long it took for a car to come by.

But that would've been immature. Right?

Now everyone just drove to the next county over; the next county that served alcohol and had a Walmart.

Still, whether the town was dead or not it still needed *her* kind of business; she was sure of it. There wasn't a single place in town where anyone could get a massage and more and more people were looking for natural treatments for their ailments. There were forty-thousand people in Morel County and some of them were bound to get sick and in need of somebody to pound on their backs and legs for half an hour.

Liza Jane Higginbotham was just the person to do the pounding. She had a lot of issues to work out.

It took her several tries to get the key to turn in the lock. When kicking, cursing, and throwing a mini tantrum with her red hair flying from her knitted cap and whipping her in the face didn't work, she turned to something else.

Liza calmed down, gave up the lock and key, said a quiet little charm to herself, and then let go of the knob and watched as the door creaked open in reluctant welcome.

"Yeah, well, you and I need to work on that," she murmured as she stepped inside.

Of course, she wouldn't *always* be able to charm it open. She'd have to figure out what made it stick and get that fixed and go about things the right way as often as she could. In the meantime, however, she was keen to explore her new building now and she didn't want to wait.

There were three rooms downstairs: a large space upfront, a bathroom, and a smaller room in the back.

The smaller room was around 10 x 20, an awkward size, and had unfortunate peeling linoleum on the floor (and smelled faintly of pickles for no discernible reason whatsoever) but she could work with it. With new floors, new paint on the walls, a privacy screen where people could change clothes, and some aromatherapy it would be a fine treatment room.

Someone had tried painting the bathroom a shocking shade of blood red, without priming it first. The original blue bled through in parts, making it look like someone really *had* splashed blood against the walls. She wasn't totally against the *Texas Chainsaw Massacre* look but figured it might not be soothing to some of her more sensitive clients.

There was also an upstairs' apartment which was available for her use as well. It consisted of a living area with a dining space in the back, a bedroom, a galley kitchen, and a bathroom that had a toilet and shower, but no sink. (The sink wasn't missing; there just wasn't enough room for one.)

Liza had no reason to live in the apartment, but she *could* use it for storage. She hoped that her actual products, as well as her services, would bring her some income. She had oils, herbs, tinctures, supplies for making one's *own* tincture, and even gemstones for sale. She'd also ordered a ton of lotions, bubble baths, creams, and organic juices and supplements. She was eager to start making her own body scrubs and shampoos, too, and stock them as well.

She used to get a kick out of making them and using what she could, giving the rest out to friends for Christmas but Mode had ridiculed her for doing it whenever he saw the opportunity.

"Why do you want to keep buying brown sugar and olive oil?" he'd ask with that condescending smirk of his. "I'm making good money now. Just go to the mall and pick out what you want. It will save you a lot of time and you're not really saving us money by doing this. I don't know why you want to do it."

What she *wanted* was to make her own damn bubble bath. She didn't care that the DIY approach wasn't saving them money, she just enjoyed it. And she secretly thought they were safer and better for her skin.

Besides, it wasn't like she had much of anything else to do anymore anyway.

She hadn't worked in years. When she'd gone back to school and received her massage therapist license she'd had a ball doing the certification and being in a classroom setting again. Liza had always liked school. Then she'd taken the job at the day spa and that had been fun, too, even though it was only part time. At least she was getting out of the house.

And her clients *liked* her.

Since she'd married Mode, most of the people she knew were *his* people. There were the bandmates, *their* girlfriends, their publicity people, their accountants, the groupies (oh God, the groupies-who would've thought a pop opera group brought groupies), and so on and so on.

She hadn't had her own people in a very, very long time. But then he'd talked her out of working at the day spa, convincing her that she'd be much happier traveling and going on the road with him. "Just think of how much fun we'll have going to South America, Scotland–Japan even! You can do whatever you want while I'm on the road!"

Starry-eyed and full of wanderlust those things *had* sounded great to her at the time. So, even though she'd paid good money to get her license, and she liked the people she worked with, she'd quit her job and let the license expire to become a stay-at-home wife who traveled with her husband.

Of course, in reality the traveling rarely happened. Sure, they'd gone on a few trips at first, and they'd had a wonderful time during those trips. Mode was a different person away from home. He was charming, knowledgeable, and relaxed. The tours were exciting. Those trips had reminded her of why she'd fallen in love with him in the first place.

But later when it came time for him to travel to San Francisco for a week he'd told her that the other members of the group were starting to complain since they couldn't bring *their* spouses with them.

"Sorry honey, but you might want to sit this one out," he'd said with concern.

"But we pay for my way, and my meals. Couldn't their spouses and girlfriends do the same? It's not like the group is paying for me to go."

He'd nodded in agreement and swore a little to show his "irritation." Then he'd said, "Let 'em simmer down a bit. Then you can come on the next one."

Of course, the next one would come around and he'd said the same thing.

"I think I'm going to get my massage license back," she'd declared one June morning, five years ago. "I've painted every single wall in the house, learned to crochet and made more afghans than I ever thought possible, and have dug around in the garden so much I'm afraid if I go any farther I might hit Hell. I need a *life*."

"I like having you at home, though," he'd all but pleaded. "You don't know how much it means to be able to come home to a place that's clean and ready for me. To know someone is inside and has food waiting. The traveling is getting old. You being there for me at home is what makes it bearable."

Liza had gathered her nerves at that point and said what had been on her mind for months. "Well maybe if I got pregnant...I mean, I think we *can* now. And I am really, really ready."

He'd looked away then, his face blank. When he'd turned back to her he'd been all smiles again. "Well, it might be hard if you're on the road. We're leaving for Bermuda next weekend and you can go with us. I was going to surprise you!"

So, for the next five tours she was "allowed" to travel with them. That had continued for a year and a half. Then it stopped again. She'd brought up pregnancy three times after that, but he'd always changed the subject. She'd finally just stopped.

In hindsight she realized that only *one* of the members had complained of her presence–the one he was currently engaged to. A trombone player. She'd been too blind to see it, or else too scared to investigate it properly.

"Serves me right," she spat.

Her voice, stronger than she'd realized, echoed in the cavernous room. It was a little thrilling. "I spent all my free time helping others see their future. I was too dim-witted to look at my *own* present."

At least she had some money. Along with the house and property, when Nana Bud died she'd left both Liza and Bryar a tidy sum from her life insurance policy and stocks she'd purchased back in the 1970s. In total, Liza Jane's part came to more than $125,000. (Which made her wonder what her grandmother had left Mabel. She'd never asked her mother.)

At one time, it would've been a fortune. Now she was going to have to make it stretch a good while to cover her expenses for at least two years, until her own business hopefully (definitely, think *positive*) took off.

So far she'd used it to rent the apartment in Beverly, move to Kentucky, get the house up and running, pay the rent for her building four months in advance, purchase all the supplies she needed to get her business up and running (massage table, products, waiting room furniture, decorations, etc.), her recertification, and to get the utilities on for everything.

And then there had been a few new outfits. Just because.

She shuddered at the amount she'd already spent.

"I *will* make this happen," she promised herself, tossing her head back so that her hair shook in the shadowy light. "This *is* going to work for me."

The overhead lights flickered off and on, a strobe-light effect from the energy that flew from the snap of her fingers.

She felt good, she felt positive.

She was going to do this, do this well, and not use any magic at all.

Oh, who was she kidding? She'd use as much as she could. A girl *had* to eat, after all.

. . .

Liza knew whose voice she'd hear on the other end of the line before she was halfway across the room. Always a glutton for punishment, she continued towards the phone all the same. It was either now or later, after all.

Mode's voice carried that pleasant, cheery tone that had irritated her so much at the end and made her swoon in the beginning.

"Hi Mode," she said carefully, and then cringed. She'd promised herself to avoid that if she could.

Nana Bud had believed that names had a tremendous amount of power attached to them, some of the greatest power that existed.

"Don't use someone's name when you're mad or flying off the handle," she'd warned her when Liza was nine and first starting to recognize the fact that she could do things that others couldn't. "If you use their name in anger, you're trapping both of you in a web you'll likely never get out of. And the same–don't say it in love unless you're real sure you mean it. That's the thing that will bind you best of all."

Still, as she spoke Mode's name aloud she was reminded of the number of times her mother had made fun of it.

"*Mode*," she'd shuddered. "That's ridiculous. It sounds too much like '*commode*.' He should at least go by a nickname. He shouldn't tempt the fates like that."

"I'm assuming you're settling in down there in little old Kudzu," he said.

Condescending prick, she said soundlessly and then watched as the book she'd left on the coffee table the night before shot up in the air and slammed back down, sending the TV remote clattering to the floor.

She was really going to have to get a grip on her emotions. Now was as good a time as any to start trying.

And maybe she should give him the benefit of the doubt. After all, her goal was to live a peaceful life that was free of stress and unwanted excitement. She could start by being civil. Besides, she couldn't be sure if he was *truly* being condescending or if it was his legitimate attempt at being cute/friendly and just sounded smarmy because she was currently pissed off at him for cheating on her and ending their marriage.

Oh, screw peaceful and relaxing, her inner mind snapped. There'd be plenty of time for that later. She'd stick with the condescension because that's just the kind of mood Mode put her in anymore.

So far in the conversation, he'd rambled on about himself for at least six minutes, giving her information about his upcoming tour and problems with the guest bathroom's pipes in her old, *their* old house.

"Lizey?" he asked, his chipper tone falling an octave. "I asked if you were settling in down there."

"Fine and dandy," she replied tightly. "I'm assuming *you're* settling into little old Jennifer."

"Jennifer's fine," he replied, not losing the smile from his voice but speaking slowly, as though speaking to an insolent child. "Are you sure you're holding up? It's an awfully big house for just one person and you're not used to being by yourself and having to do things alone."

Except for all those weeks you went off and left me alone while you were on tour, she mentally snapped back at him. "I'm fine," she replied instead. "I like being by myself. At least I know I am in good company."

"But still...you know you can always come back up here when you're ready. Your mom or sister will be sure to take you in and help you."

Every hair on Liza's head rose to angry attention. *You don't even know who I am*, she wanted to scream at the top of her lungs. *You never let me be myself so you don't know what I am capable of! Don't you remember? Don't you remember that first year and what...?*

Her silence appeared to make him nervous. "Is there anything I can do for you on my end? Any way I can help you with, you know, official business?"

What he *really* wanted to know was if he could do anything to help her clear the rest of her part of their storage unit out faster. If he could do anything to stop the loose ends of mail she figured were still being delivered to his house. If there was anything he could do to speed up the divorce process...

He was asking if he could do anything to help cut their ties to each other quicker.

"Not a darn thing," she said. "I'm moving just as fast as I can."

"Oh! I know you are! I didn't mean to imply that you were dragging your heels or anything," he said smoothly.

Yeah, the way you didn't drag your heels when you invited your mistress to move in with you before I'd even packed my suitcase, she thought wryly.

"Now we'll be out of town for all of next month," he said. "I'm going on tour with the group and we have sixteen dates on the west coast. So if there's anything you need from up here– "

"You telling me so that I can come up then and you two won't have to run into me?" she finished for him. "Because I can tell you now that I won't be coming up there until after Christmas, probably. I have to start working on my business this week. I have men coming in next week to start construction and I can't leave them alone without any supervision."

Liza, who'd sat through most of the conversation feeling a bit depressed, straightened her back now, proud at how official she'd sounded. *Ha! Take that. I have work, too!*

"No! That's not what I meant at all. I just meant that Larry and Sheila next door have the spare key," he replied, his voice beginning to sound a little strained.

Liza was now confused. Her mind began to spin as she traveled backwards in time to the incident involving the house key and the ensuing argument. "Well, I still have my key. Remember? I tried to return it to you and you wouldn't accept it. You brought it to my apartment and said that I needed to keep it until everything was final, until the house was completely in your name."

"Yes, well, we um..." Mode let his voice trail off his until his end of the line fell uncomfortably silent. It was in the silence that the implication of what he was saying struck Liza square in the middle of the forehead.

Damn her third eye.

"You had the locks changed," she accused him, unable to keep the high pitch of anger from creeping into her voice. "Well I'll be damned."

Mode coughed nervously and through the line she could see the tips of his ears, rosy from the anxiety he was feeling. Soon he'd be unbuttoning the top of his shirt. *Good.* "It's just that there's been a lot of thefts in the neighborhood recently and–"

Enjoying his discomfort more than any decent person should, Liza allowed him to ramble while she closed her eyes and let herself drift hundreds of miles away and back in time.

On the movie screen behind her eyelids she could see them a few days ago, the catalyst for the current conversation.

There was Mode, with his stubby beard, tweed jacket he'd picked up at Goodwill, and red suspenders that she'd always thought looked ridiculous but kept quiet about because she didn't want to hurt his feelings.

And then there was Jennifer, pacing around the living room like a caged cat in her black tights and deep orange tunic sweeping her knees. Her voice was controlled but her skinny little shoulders were hunched forward, and her eyes were bright with blue-tinted rage. "I don't want that *woman* to have a key to my house Mode."

"She's not 'that woman' Jen. Liza's a great girl. She'd never do anything to hurt you or us!" Mode, who abhorred conflict, looked crushed. His eyes were lowered to the travertine tile Eliza had installed two years earlier and his mouth dropped at the corners–the way it got when he thought the world was stacked against him.

"She's vindictive and mean-spirited and I don't trust her as far as I can throw her," Jennifer spat. "Change the locks!"

Liza chuckled at the scene playing out before her eyes on her own private movie screen.

She was the vindictive one who couldn't be trusted? She hadn't been the one to make it her goal to sleep with a married man on a twelve-city tour and document the affair in Instagram posts.

Liza still couldn't believe they'd carried on that affair as long as they had without her knowing. When he'd told her about the Starbucks girl and that he was moving out, she'd thought he'd gone insane. Insanity she could fix. But when she learned he was actually leaving her for someone he worked with, that was different. That was serious. That's when she knew she'd lost him.

Mode was still babbling some nonsense when she interrupted him. "Sorry, I've got something on the stove. I'd better go."

"What? You're cooking! That's great. I am so glad that you're—"

She'd never know which part of her cooking made him "glad" because she hung up before he finished.

Eh well, she shrugged as she stared at the blue light on her phone's screen.

Perhaps she *was* a little vindictive. After all, she hadn't made an entirely innocent exit from their house. With Bryar at her side, begging Liza to let her curse something or put out a good hex, she'd loosened some things in all the toilets so that they'd overflow and run for the entire two weeks that the happy couple was on vacation, removed the new thermostat which effectively left them without air or heat until they could call someone in to replace it, and then removed all the towel racks and light bulbs and taken them with her.

Just for the fun of it.

. . .

The last of her boxes were unpacked.

Liza's meager personal belongings were either neatly stowed away in closets or arranged on bookshelves and credenzas throughout her grandparents' house.

Her house.

She wasn't sure it would ever completely be *hers*, but she knew she belonged there.

Liza didn't bring much with her. The few items she'd deemed important enough to transport from Boston were sentimental and random. In fact, from the looks of some of the things she packed, Liza was now worried she might have unknowingly suffered from some kind of mental breakdown before she left. Her belongings had clearly not been chosen by someone who was in full control of their decision-making and cognitive skills.

For instance, she hadn't brought a single cup or plate or towel with her yet somehow managed to carefully pack the collection of foreign Coca-Cola bottles she'd gathered during their international travels. They were now artfully displayed on a library table in the living room.

She'd forgotten to pack any underwear (and, since all her drawers were empty when she left the house, had no idea where they were, which was a little disturbing) but *had* packed a box of nothing but melted candle wax that she'd collected from all the candle holders in the house. Yes, she liked to melt down the old and make new candles but why had she deemed *that* wax necessary?

And then there was the plastic bag full of more than three-hundred corks.

Still, she'd managed to bring every single item of clothing she'd ever owned, including the sweatshirt she'd cut the neck out of back in 1989 when she was just a kid. Well, other than her underwear. *That*, she'd managed to leave...somewhere.

"Liza Jane," she declared, her voice booming through the empty rooms. "You're a little pathetic."

The dryer buzzed in response, a reminder that she needed to change loads. The sheets and blankets on the bed were clean, but musty from non-use over the past few years. She'd spent the previous night coughing and sneezing. She wasn't ready to throw them out yet so she hoped a good dousing with Tide and that fabric softener with the annoying white teddy bear who was always laughing would help.

Momentarily forgetting her self-deprecating speech to herself, Liza scurried to the dryer to take action. With each thing she'd done that morning, she'd mentally hit Mode over the head with it.

He didn't think she could hack it. *He* didn't think she'd stay down there. *He* didn't think she could be alone.

Liza Jane was a stress cleaner. She enjoyed dusting, washing dishes, mopping, and organizing. It just wasn't cutting it today, though. The more she thought about Mode's phone call, the madder she got.

Thinking about Mode frolicking around her house with Jennifer did not help. Changing her locks. Ha! Like a lock could keep *her* out.

Mode would've known that, too.

Oh, he *knew* she was a witch. He was embarrassed by it, but he knew. "Just don't do anything out in public, okay?" He hadn't even had the decency to look ashamed or embarrassed when he'd asked.

"Like what, Darren?" she'd snapped. "Ride my broom? Turn the waiter into a frog?"

She'd looked at his face then and saw that it wasn't awkwardness of her abilities that had him humiliated, it was old-fashioned fear. He was afraid of her. She'd softened a little then and changed the subject after promising him she wouldn't make a public spectacle of herself.

Hours later something must have clicked inside and he'd felt guilty. As a peace offering, he'd brought her a broom, one of those old-fashioned ones that looked handmade and like it belonged by a storybook witch's front door.

In fact, it *was* now standing by her front door. She was sentimental, after all. And it was a nice broom.

Still, his ideas never wavered. Two years later he asked her to move her altar out of their bedroom and into another room of the house. He claimed it was for the sake of "space" but she'd read him like a book. It was easy to do it by then. She only had to lightly press her thumbs together. She'd pressed them on his temples once, and then on his third eye, and they'd been connected ever since and would be forever.

Until *she* ended it.

"Well, shit," she sighed, looking around her living room again.

Her face cooled just a fraction and she closed her eyes to gather herself together again. She was angry at herself, angry for allowing him into this space, for making her angry *here*. Somewhere that had nothing to do with him. This space was meant to be hers and she'd all but invited him inside and asked him to throw darts at her.

It wasn't fair. Why couldn't her life be fair for a change? She'd given up years of it for his career. She'd helped put him through that last year of school, the year his parents died and their account (and subsequently his college funding) had been frozen.

She'd dropped out herself to work two jobs so that he could start his business and had then traveled all over the world with him so that he could work with the pop opera group and feel "fulfilled." She had put off having children because he wasn't ready, let her massage license expire so that he could have someone at home, kept the house clean, hired the maintenance workers, kept his records and balanced the checkbook, hid her magic and–

Liza, in the midst of her depressing and angry march down Memory Lane had not counted on the fact that the house could read her thoughts. She wouldn't make *that* mistake again.

Before she'd finished her last thought, two things happened at once:

The front door swung open from the pressure of a hearty knock...

And two of the foreign Coca-Cola bottles sailed off the shelf on the other side of the room, hovered dramatically in the air before proceeding to spin around uncontrollably, and then crashed to the ground, showering the living room with a thousand glittery shards of glass.

Liza, hand covering her mouth in embarrassment, was left staring at her visitor in shock.

"Um, hi?"

The curly-haired brunette holding a corning ware dish covered in aluminum foil gave her a baffled grin. "I'm your neighbor from the next farm over. Um, welcome to Kudzu Valley?"

AVAILABLE NOW!

Made in the USA
Middletown, DE
06 December 2020

26400603R00093